*Who Is Jesus?*

# WHO IS JESUS?

*Disputed Questions and Answers*

Carl E. Braaten

*William B. Eerdmans Publishing Company*

*Grand Rapids, Michigan / Cambridge, U.K.*

Published 2011 by

Wm. B. Eerdmans Publishing Co.

2140 Oak Industrial Drive N.E., Grand Rapids, Michigan 49505 /
P.O. Box 163, Cambridge CB3 9PU U.K.

Printed in the United States of America

17  16  15  14  13  12  11        7  6  5  4  3  2  1

**Library of Congress Cataloging-in-Publication Data**

Braaten, Carl E., 1929-

Who is Jesus?: disputed questions and answers / Carl E. Braaten.

p.      cm.

ISBN 978-0-8028-6668-4 (pbk.: alk. paper)

1. Jesus Christ — Person and offices — Miscellanea.

2. Apologetics — Miscellanea.   I. Title.

BT203.B73   2011

232'.8  — dc23

2011026642

www.eerdmans.com

# Contents

# Contents

# By Way of Introduction

The aim of apologetic theology is to provide answers to disputed questions. The most disputed questions in theology today have to do with Jesus of Nazareth. Who was Jesus? Historical-critical research into the beginnings of Christianity has been frustrated by endless attempts to explain who Jesus was and what he said and did. No scholarly consensus exists regarding the question that Jesus addressed to his disciples on the road to Caesarea Philippi, "Who do you say that I am?" (Matt. 16:15). For centuries, indeed, for more than a millennium, Christian theologians believed they possessed the definitive answer in the Nicene Creed: "We believe in one Lord, Jesus Christ, the only Son of God, eternally begotten of the Father, God from God, Light from Light, true God from true God, begotten, not made, of one Being with the Father." That is what I believe and confess along with all other orthodox Christians. But that does not in itself answer the question of how to explain the development from the Jesus of the Gospels to the Christ of the Creeds. How did the Jesus of history become the Christ of faith?

The use of the modern historical-critical method gave rise to suspicion, especially in scholarly circles, that Jesus was the most misunderstood personality of all time. A shift took place from a dogmatic approach to a thoroughgoing historical perspective. Scholars wanted to discover who Jesus "really" was in his own time and place and not merely accept at face value what his followers believed about him. Thus began "the quest of the historical Jesus" that Albert Schweitzer (1875-1965) wrote about in his monumental classic by that title.[1] The original quest that started with Hermann Samuel Reimarus (1694-1768) and continued until Schweitzer gave way to a new quest led by New Testament scholars such as Ernst Käsemann (1906-1998), Günther Bornkamm (1905-1990),

---

1. On the three quests for the historical Jesus, see chapter 1 below.

and others. That quest came to an end with the waning influence of the theology of Rudolf Bultmann (1884-1976).

A third quest is now underway, conducted chiefly by New Testament scholars in Britain and the United States. Many of them are in fundamental disagreement with each other. Just to give an example: the Gospel research of a conservative scholar like N. T. "Tom" Wright (1948-) is in many respects the polar opposite of that of a liberal scholar like John Dominic Crossan (1934-). Tom Wright believes that the results of his study support and vindicate the Christology of the ancient church, defined by the Councils of Nicaea and Chalcedon. John Dominic Crossan believes, along with other scholars of the "Jesus Seminar," that the results of critical historiography undercut the christological dogmas of the church.

I have entitled this book "Who *Is* Jesus?" rather than "Who *Was* Jesus?" because it is written from the standpoint of the Christian belief that Jesus is not merely a past historical figure but is now alive and embodied in the church through its means of grace. The first chapter will show why I am as deeply suspicious of the claims to scientific objectivity of the new questers as Schweitzer was of the original questers. All of them tend to discover a Jesus created in their own image. Some of them use their reconstruction of the historical Jesus to attack what they do not like about the institutional church. Others find continuity between the life and ministry of Jesus and the message of apostolic Christianity.

In this book I am returning to the subject of my doctoral dissertation written under the supervision of Paul Tillich (1886-1965) at Harvard University. The subject was Martin Kähler's (1835-1912) exposure of the fallacies involved in the attempt of modern critical scholarship to discover the real Jesus of history.[2] He dubbed it "the so-called historical Jesus."[3] I agreed with Kähler that the modern search for the historical Jesus has been a failure. By the same criteria the current quest must be deemed a

---

2. The title of my doctoral dissertation is *Christ, Faith, and History, An Inquiry into the Meaning of Martin Kähler's Distinction between the Historical Jesus and the Biblical Christ Developed in Its Past and Present Contexts* (Harvard University, Cambridge, Massachusetts, 1959).

3. See Martin Kähler, *The So-Called Historical Jesus and the Historic Biblical Christ*, trans. and ed. with an Introduction by Carl E. Braaten (Philadelphia: Fortress Press, 1964).

failure, whether carried out by the more positive or the more negative critics. The idea of the search presupposes that the real Jesus has been lost and needs to be found. My view is that the only real Jesus is the One presented in the canonical Gospels and that any other Jesus is irrelevant to Christian faith.

The title of each of the chapters poses a question which has engaged many of the greatest minds in the history of Christian theology. They have not given us simple pat answers that we have only to repeat. Every theologian has to struggle with them in his or her own way. The answers I have given will reflect not only that I stand broadly within the tradition of Lutheran theology but also indicate which theologians in the history of Christianity have influenced my thinking the most. My hope is that what I have written will stimulate people to find their own answers, perhaps better ones, to the disputed questions concerning the identity and meaning of Jesus of Nazareth. For me the secret of learning in theology has always been to challenge the answers great minds have given to disputed questions and to struggle for more adequate ones, faithful to Scripture and church tradition and relevant to the Christian faith and its message for our time.

## · I ·

# *What Can We Know*
# *about Jesus of Nazareth?*

C hristianity stands or falls with what it knows about Jesus of Nazareth. If, for example, it could be proved that Jesus never existed, that
would presumably spell the end of the Christian faith. For there can be
no Christianity without Jesus. Similarly, if the leading scholars of the "Jesus Seminar" were correct in claiming that the first evangelists and apostles produced a false picture of Jesus, that would discredit the church's
appeal to the New Testament. Many critical historians are convinced
that the first Christians misinterpreted the intentions of Jesus and that
now for the first time it is possible, by virtue of new sources and methods, to discover who Jesus really was and what he actually said and did.
Such a reconstructed image of Jesus, it is imagined, should give rise to a
new Christianity for these modern times. I refer to such scholars as negative critics.

On the other hand, many of the best biblical scholars are convinced
that the picture of Jesus that we have in the Gospels, especially Matthew,
Mark, and Luke, is quite reliable, based on eyewitness reports, and thus
true to the way he was remembered by his earliest followers. They see no
need to call for a revision of historic Christianity, its fundamental beliefs
and creeds. I refer to such scholars as positive critics.

The negative and positive critics are both engaged in a new quest of
the historical Jesus. They agree that the modern quest for the real Jesus
of history is historically possible, religiously important, and even theo-
logically necessary. Their motives are decidedly different and they reach

quite opposite conclusions. But both sides aim to discover who Jesus really was by using the modern critical methods of historical research. The negative critics believe that the results will pull the rug out from under traditional Christianity. The positive critics believe that the results will rather support the mainstream of the Christian tradition. Liberals and radicals tend to favor the first option, conservatives and traditionalists more naturally the second. N. T. Wright, a prominent British New Testament theologian and Anglican bishop, calls the new quest the "third quest." The new questers address the question: "Is the Jesus of history also the Christ of faith, and is the Christ of faith also the Jesus of history?" The negative critics say "no," appealing to the results of modern historical science. The positive critics say "yes," and aim to prove it by using the same methods. If the same question can be answered in a positive sense by better historico-scientific research, then faith and knowledge can be reconciled in our time. N. T. Wright, one of the positive critics and one of the leaders of the new quest, writes,

> The church has no vested interest in preventing people coming up with new ideas about Jesus. Indeed, I shall myself be arguing that . . . the real, historical Jesus still has many surprises in store for institutional Christianity. . . . It is possible to take current questions seriously and still emerge with a way of understanding Jesus that does justice both to history and to mainstream Christian belief. . . . It is certainly not true that I have "found" a "Jesus" who has merely reinforced the belief-system I had before the process began. The closer I get to Jesus within his historical context, the more I find my previous ideas, and indeed my previous self, radically subverted.[1]

This to and fro of scholarly opinion about Jesus has a long history that goes back to the eighteenth century. Then for the first time biblical scholars dared to break free of the dogmatic controls applied during the heyday of Protestant Orthodoxy. As long as the traditional belief in the plenary inspiration of the Bible and its verbal inerrancy held sway, schol-

---

1. N. T. Wright, *Who Was Jesus?* (Grand Rapids: Wm. B. Eerdmans Publishing Co., 1992), viii.

ars did not question the historical trustworthiness of the Bible. The idea that the Bible contained any inaccuracies or contradictions was simply unthinkable, given the belief that the Holy Spirit dictated the very words of the Bible. To clinch the point, it was said, "the Holy Spirit does not contradict himself."

## The First Quest of the Historical Jesus

An uncritical attitude toward the Bible changed with the rise of rationalism among the free-thinkers of the Enlightenment.[2] Hermann Samuel Reimarus (1694-1768), a professor of ancient Semitic languages at Hamburg University, was credited by Albert Schweitzer with having begun the modern "quest of the historical Jesus."[3] Reimarus drove a wedge between Jesus and Christianity, portraying Jesus as a failed revolutionary and Christianity as a hoax founded on a mistaken belief in his resurrection. Not wishing to return to fishing, Jesus' disciples stole his body and then circulated stories that he was alive. Once the cork was out of the bottle, rationalistic historians invented a slew of naturalistic theories to account for everything supernatural in the Gospel reports about Jesus.

Another rationalist, Heinrich Eberhard Gottlob Paulus (1761-1851), wrote a biography of Jesus in which he explained (away) all the miracles in a way that conforms to the laws of nature. For Paulus the feeding of the five thousand was a matter of Jesus and his disciples sharing their lunch with those who had none, inspiring others to do the same, until all were fed. David Friedrich Strauss (1808-1874) invented a mythological explanation of the miracles. The miracle stories were myths narrated as historical events. Strauss left little of the historical content in the Gospels. Instead, what counted was the eternally valid idea of "God-manhood"[4] expressed in the story of Jesus; whether as myth or history makes no difference.

2. The "Enlightenment" refers to an eighteenth-century philosophical movement in Europe that placed its trust primarily in reason, fostering a spirit of skepticism over against the authority of tradition.

3. Cf. Albert Schweitzer, *The Quest of the Historical Jesus* (New York: The Macmillan Co., 1961).

4. This was Hegel's term for the incarnation.

When Schweitzer wrote his classic account of the quest of the historical Jesus early in the twentieth century, he had no idea that he was planting the seeds of skepticism regarding the entire project. Schweitzer charged that all the biographers of Jesus put their own thoughts into the mouth of Jesus, touting their findings as the result of pure historical research.[5] They painted a picture of Jesus that matched their own ideas about religion and morality. In short, they modernized Jesus. Not much has changed since Schweitzer's negative verdict. The quest of the historical Jesus is back in full swing. Its practitioners are making the same claim to objectivity. And the rediscovered Jesus often becomes a function of artful ventriloquism. But with this remark we are getting ahead of our story.

Writing at about the same time, Martin Kähler (1835-1912) reached the same conclusion as Schweitzer. Kähler rejected the Enlightenment project to discover the real Jesus of history from behind the Gospel texts.[6] He said, "The historical Jesus of modern authors conceals from us the living Christ.... I regard the entire Life-of-Jesus movement as a blind alley."[7] In the judgment of both Schweitzer and Kähler, the Jesus scholars found in the personality of Jesus the reflections of their own ideas and ideals. Adolf von Harnack (1851-1930), a great church historian and a contemporary of Schweitzer and Kähler, created a picture of Jesus in harmony with modern liberal Protestantism, whose cardinal beliefs were the fatherhood of God, the brotherhood of man, and the infinite value of each individual soul.[8] To that George Tyrell (1861-1909) responded: "The Christ that Harnack sees, looking back through nineteen centuries of Catholic darkness, is only the reflection of a liberal Protestant face, seen at the bottom of a deep well.... Whatever Jesus was, he was in no sense a Liberal Protestant."[9]

---

5. Schweitzer, *The Quest of the Historical Jesus*, pp. 398-99.

6. Martin Kähler, *The So-Called Historical Jesus and the Historic Biblical Christ*, tr. with an introduction by Carl E. Braaten (Philadelphia: Fortress Press, 1964).

7. Kähler, *The So-Called Historical Jesus*, pp. 43, 46.

8. Adolf von Harnack, *What Is Christianity?* tr. Thomas Bailey Saunders (New York: Harper & Brothers, 1957), pp. 19-75. The German edition is entitled *Das Wesen des Christentums*, published in 1901.

9. George Tyrell, *Christianity at the Crossroads* (London: Longmans Green, 1909), p. 49.

Protestant theologians who cared about the integrity of the Christian message capitalized on the growing mood of historical skepticism. Around 1920, members of the school of dialectical theology[10] — Karl Barth (1886-1968), Emil Brunner (1889-1966), Friedrich Gogarten (1887-1968), Rudolf Bultmann, and Paul Tillich (1886-1965) — disclaimed the "historical Jesus" of modern scholarship. They found support for their rejection in the statement of the apostle Paul, "Even though we once regarded Christ from a human point of view *(kata sarka),* we regard him thus no longer" (2 Cor. 5:16). The Jesus-questers can at best lay claim to some always debatable knowledge of the Christ according to the flesh *(kata sarka).* But that is not the living Christ of the missionary proclamation of Paul and the other apostles. The dialectical theologians agreed that the historical Jesus of the modern biographers is not the biblical Christ; he is not the Christ of faith. In the early 1920s Emil Brunner wrote: "The question whether Jesus ever existed will always hover upon the margin of history as a possibility, in spite of the protest of theologians, and of the liberal theologians in particular. Even the bare fact of the existence of Christ as an historical person is not assured."[11] Hardly less severe was Paul Tillich's judgment that "seen in the light of its basic intention, the attempt of historical criticism to find the empirical truth about Jesus of Nazareth was a failure. The historical Jesus, namely, the Jesus behind the symbols of his reception as the Christ, not only did not appear but receded farther and farther with every new step."[12] Karl Barth stated that the "life of Jesus" research, whether conducted by liberal or conservative biblical critics, is not worthy of theological consideration. He said, "There is no reason why historical-critical Bible research should be . . . chasing the ghost of an historical Jesus in the vacuum behind the New Testament."[13]

---

10. Cf. *A Map of Twentieth Century Theology,* ed. Carl E. Braaten and Robert W. Jenson (Minneapolis: Fortress Press, 1995), pp. 39-61.

11. Emil Brunner, *The Mediator,* tr. Olive Wyon (Philadelphia: The Westminster Press, 1947), pp. 186-87.

12. Paul Tillich, *Systematic Theology* (Chicago: The University of Chicago Press, 1957), vol. II, p. 102.

13. Karl Barth, *Church Dogmatics,* vol. I, part 2, tr. G. T. Thomson and Harold Knight (New York: Charles Scribner's Sons, 1956), pp. 64-65.

The dialectical theologians were influenced not only by the combined judgments of Schweitzer and Kähler but also by the writings of Søren Kierkegaard (1813-1855). Kierkegaard approached the problem of the historical Jesus from the standpoint of faith. Kierkegaard asked, "Can there be an historical point of departure for a consciousness that is eternal in quality? How can such a point of departure be more than of historical interest? Can eternal salvation be built on historical knowledge?"[14] Kierkegaard argued that historical knowledge never yields anything more than approximate certainty and that a person's eternal destiny must not be based on a mere probability. Kähler also questioned whether the assurance of faith can be made dependent on the always oscillating results of historical research. This was his question: How can the results of scholarly inquiry into the life of the historical Jesus create the basis and contents of the Christian faith? Paul Tillich wrote: "I do not believe that Kähler's answer to the question of the historical Jesus is sufficient for our situation today, especially in view of the problem of demythologization and the ensuing discussions. But I do believe that one emphasis in Kähler's answer is decisive for our present situation, namely, the necessity to make the certainty of faith independent of the unavoidable uncertainties of historical research. Finding the way in which this can be done for our time is one of the main tasks of contemporary theology."[15] This chapter on our knowledge of the historical Jesus is an attempt to undertake this unfinished task.

Thomas Jefferson (1743-1826) was one of the founding fathers of the United States, a man much revered as the author of the Declaration of Independence. He has been hailed as a great Christian patriot. One of his biographers wrote that he was perhaps the most self-consciously theological of all American presidents. He was born an Anglican, but even as a boy he began to doubt fundamental Anglican beliefs, like the Trinity, incarnation, atonement, resurrection, original sin, and salvation by faith, as well as all the miracles of Jesus. But he liked Jesus, that is, the picture of Jesus produced by the rationalistic historians of the Enlightenment.

14. Quoted from Hermann Diem, *Dogmatics,* tr. Harold Knight (Edinburgh: Oliver & Boyd, Ltd., 1959), p. 9. The questions above are a paraphrase of what Kierkegaard wrote.
15. Paul J. Tillich, foreword in Kähler, *The So-Called Historical Jesus,* p. xii.

He agreed that to get back to the real Jesus and his true teachings it is necessary to separate the wheat from the chaff. Jefferson re-wrote the Gospels, anticipating the approach of the scholars of the fashionable "Jesus Seminar." The chaff was all the unbelievable supernatural stuff and the wheat was the common-sensical moral teachings of Jesus. Jefferson called his bowdlerized edition of the Gospels, "The Life and Morals of Jesus of Nazareth,"[16] picturing Jesus in line with New England transcendental deism. He used the cut-and-paste method, excising the passages that he regarded as vulgar ignorance, superstition, fanaticism, and fabrication. Yet, Jefferson professed that he was a Christian, in the only way that it made sense to an enlightened person, and that is to accept the religion *of* Jesus and not the religion *about* Jesus. Jefferson did not draw the only possible logical inference that such a view would at best make him some kind of a Jew rather than a believer in Christ.

## Theological Criticism of the Quest

*Abusus non tollit usum.*[17] Kähler and the dialectical theologians were not expressing disinterest in Jesus of Nazareth as he was remembered and portrayed by the New Testament evangelists and apostles. They were calling into question the attempt to discover the real historical Jesus behind the Gospel texts. Everything depends on what counts as really "historical." Martin Kähler played on two different German words for history, *Historie* and *Geschichte*. The two words were used in the title of his book, *Der sogenannte historische Jesus und der geschichtliche biblische Christus.* Kähler intended to distinguish between the historical *(historische)* Jesus of the critical historiographers and the historic *(geschichtliche)* Jesus who is the Christ of the Bible. The *historische Jesus* was the reconstructed Jesus of the critics; the *geschichtliche Christus* was Jesus seen in terms of his historic significance.

Kähler asked, "What is actually a real historical event?"[18] The real Je-

---

16. Thomas Jefferson, *The Life and Morals of Jesus of Nazareth* (Washington: Government Printing Office, 1904).

17. "Wrong use does not preclude proper use."

18. "Was ist eigentlich eine geschichtliche grösse?"

sus of history is not the excavated bones of a dead man lying in the rubble of history, often re-presented by critical historians as mis-taken, misquoted, and mis-understood. Kähler dismissed the "so-called historical Jesus" as having no real significance for Christian faith. On the contrary, the real Jesus of history is the Man of Nazareth who initiated a chain reaction of events, whose words and deeds were remembered and celebrated within a living stream of tradition that lasts to this day.

The whole Christ of the whole Bible is none other than Jesus of Nazareth who lived, preached, died, and rose from the grave, anticipated as the coming Messiah in the Old Testament and experienced as the living Word in the New Testament church. For Kähler and the dialectical theologians, the real Jesus "was crucified, died, and was buried," and he is now alive in the Word of preaching, as *kerygma*. *Kerygma* is the Greek New Testament word for the preaching of the gospel of Jesus Christ by the apostles. Kähler appropriated this word to make his point that the real Jesus is the Christ of apostolic preaching. The kerygmatic Christ is Jesus of Nazareth under a new mode of existence. The risen Jesus is Christ proclaimed. For Kähler the real Jesus is the One who meets us as the Word of God, through the Scriptures and the *kerygma* of the church. Jesus can be encountered now as the living Christ of faith, and not as a figure of history reconstructed by scholars who imagine ever new hypotheses to explain what really happened, in contrast to what the Gospel texts report.

To be clear, Kähler did not separate the early Christian *kerygma* from the historic *(geschichtliche)* figure of Jesus. The Christ of faith and the real Jesus of history are one and the same, so that it is equally appropriate to speak of the Jesus of faith and the Christ of history. Faith is not interested in a Christ-*kerygma* identifiable without reference to Jesus of Nazareth. But could it not happen that a new school of theology might arise that separates Jesus and the *kerygma*? Some of Rudolf Bultmann's critics accused him of doing just that. Bultmann started his theological career as a dialectical theologian and ally of Karl Barth. Later came a parting of their ways. However, before Bultmann initiated his program of "demythologizing" the New Testament,[19] he seemed to be on the right track. He

19. Rudolf Bultmann shook the theological world by proposing to eliminate the myth-

took up Kähler's insight that the real Christ is the preached (kerygmatic) Christ. Bultmann wrote:

> The crucified and resurrected Christ encounters us in the Word of preaching, and never in any other way. It would surely be a mistake if one here wanted to inquire back into the historical origin of preaching, as if this could demonstrate its rightness. That would mean to want to establish faith in the Word of God by historical inquiry. The Word of preaching encounters us here as the Word of God over against which we cannot put the question of legitimation, but it asks us whether or not we will believe it.[20]

Here Bultmann is reinforcing Kähler's idea that, if Christians had to wait for scholars to reach a consensus about the "historical Jesus" in order to meet him for the first time,[21] they would either have to wait forever, or the modern historical critic would assume the role of an apostle.

Bultmann's critics accused him of writing ambiguous things about the relation of Jesus to the *kerygma*. On the one hand he could write, "The content of the message *(kerygma)* is thus an event, a historical fact, the appearance of Jesus of Nazareth, his birth but at the same time his work, his death, and his resurrection. . . . Christian preaching is the communication of a historical fact."[22] If that was not enough to assure his readers that he believed Jesus of Nazareth is indispensable to the *kerygma*, he wrote this: "I do not deny that the resurrection *kerygma* is

---

ological elements in the New Testament in order to understand its message. He claimed that the biblical three-storied universe and belief in angels were elements of primitive mythology incredible in the modern world. See Bultmann, "New Testament and Mythology," in *Kerygma and Myth*, ed. Hans W. Bartsch, tr. Reginald H. Fuller (London: S.P.C.K., 1954).

20. Rudolf Bultmann, "Offenbarung und Heilsgeschehen," in *Beiträge zur evangelischen Theologie*, ed. Ernst Wolf (Munich: Evangelischer Verlag, Albert Lampp, 1941), pp. 7, 66.

21. Cf. the arrogant claim of Marcus Borg, one of the more interesting gnostics of our time, that thanks to his historical research he was *Meeting Jesus Again for the First Time*, which was the title of his book (San Francisco: HarperSanFrancisco, 1994).

22. Rudolf Bultmann, "Preaching: Genuine and Secularized," in *Religion and Culture: Essays in Honor of Paul Tillich*, ed. Walter Leibrecht (New York: Harper & Brothers, 1959), p. 240.

firmly rooted to the earthly figure of the crucified Jesus."[23] Kähler could not have said it any more clearly. The *kerygma* hinges on a historical event, the sheer facticity of Jesus and his death on the cross. Bultmann realized that if the *kerygma* loses its attachment to Jesus, it evaporates into a celestial myth. On the other hand, Bultmann's unclarity about the place of the historical Jesus in the *kerygma* of the New Testament gave rise to the new (the second) quest of the historical Jesus.

## The Second Quest of the Historical Jesus

Bultmann's most celebrated pupils (Ernst Käsemann, Günther Born-kamm, and others) became dissatisfied with his waffling on the relation between history, faith, and the *kerygma*. Bultmann's chief contribution as a New Testament historian was to have applied the method of form criticism[24] in his study of the Synoptic Gospels. His aim was to analyze the earliest oral traditions about Jesus before they were written down. The effect of form criticism was to increase doubt as to whether the Gospel texts were accurately based on firsthand memories of what Jesus said and did. Thus Bultmann offered this famous dictum: "I do indeed think that we can know almost nothing concerning the life and personality of Jesus, since the early Christian sources show no interest in either, are moreover fragmentary and legendary; and other sources about Jesus do not exist."[25]

In reaction to Bultmann, Käsemann published an essay entitled "The Problem of the Historical Jesus" in which he called for a renewal of the quest.[26] After that a flood of books and articles on Jesus appeared, written by Bornkamm, Ernst Fuchs, Gerhard Ebeling, Hans Conzelmann, Herbert

---

23. Rudolf Bultmann, "Reply to the Theses of J. Schniewind," in *Kerygma and Myth*, p. 112.

24. Form criticism was first developed by Hermann Gunkel to classify various literary patterns in the Old Testament.

25. Rudolf Bultmann, *Jesus and the Word*, tr. Louise P. Smith and Ermine H. Lantero (New York: Charles Scribner's Sons, 1934), p. 9.

26. Ernst Käsemann, "The Problem of the Historical Jesus," in *Essays on New Testament Themes*, tr. W. J. Montague (London: SCM Press, 1964), pp. 15-47.

Braun, James Robinson, and many others.[27] No one at that time was suggesting a return to the old quest of the nineteenth-century rationalistic and romantic biographers, with their interest in chronology, topography, and psychology. Rather, the new questers were worried about the lack of material continuity between the historical Jesus and the kerygmatic Christ in Bultmann's existentialist hermeneutics. The new questers wanted to reassert the constitutive significance of Jesus of Nazareth for Christian faith. Käsemann wrote: "Christian faith is here (i.e., in Bultmann's theology of the New Testament) being understood as faith in the exalted Lord, for which the Jesus of history as such is no longer considered of decisive importance."[28] For Käsemann, the Christ of the Easter *kerygma* must be continuous with the Jesus of history; the validity of preaching and faith depends on it. Anything less than that is docetism, the ancient heresy that substituted a heavenly being in place of the flesh-and-blood Man from Nazareth. Käsemann feared that the Easter faith would dissolve into mythology if the risen Christ were not identical with the earthly Jesus.

Like Käsemann, Günther Bornkamm felt keenly the deficiency of Bultmann's treatment of the historical Jesus. So he wrote a short monograph on Jesus,[29] the only one of Bultmann's pupils to dare such a project after Schweitzer's and Kähler's devastating critiques of the nineteenth-century biographies. In Bultmann's theology, Bornkamm wrote, "Jesus Christ has become a mere saving fact and has ceased to be a person. He himself has no longer any history."[30] Bornkamm conceded that neither the sources nor the methods available for Gospel research offer much promise of laying bare the facts of history to establish what actually happened. Yet the point of the new quest was to show that the pre-Easter

27. Günther Bornkamm, *Jesus of Nazareth*, tr. James M. Robinson (New York: Harper & Brothers, 1959); Ernst Fuchs, *Studies of the Historical Jesus*, tr. Andrew Scobie (London: SCM Press, 1964); Gerhard Ebeling, "Jesus and Faith," in *Word and Faith*, tr. James W. Leitch (Philadelphia: Fortress Press, 1963); Hans Conzelmann, *Jesus* (Philadelphia: Fortress Press, 1973); Herbert Braun, *Jesus. Der Man aus Nazareth und seine Zeit* (Tübingen: J. C. B. Mohr, 1984); James M. Robinson, *A New Quest of the Historical Jesus* (London: SCM Press, 1959).

28. Käsemann, "The Problem of the Historical Jesus," p. 16.

29. Bornkamm, *Jesus of Nazareth*.

30. Günther Bornkamm, "Myth and Gospel," in *Kerygma and History*, tr. and ed. Carl E. Braaten and Roy A. Harrisville (Nashville: Abingdon Press, 1962), p. 186.

stage of the tradition about Jesus was consistent with the post-Easter recollections of Jesus in the *kerygma,* that is, to show that history and *kerygma* are interpenetrating in the Gospels. Bornkamm wrote: "In every layer, therefore, and in each individual part, the tradition is witness of the reality of Jesus' history and the reality of his resurrection. Our task, then, is to seek the history in the *kerygma* of the Gospels, and in this history to seek the *kerygma.*"[31]

Ernst Fuchs (1903-1983) and Gerhard Ebeling (1912-2001) linked their inquiries into the historical Jesus to their specific hermeneutical theories about the connections between language and faith. They had no interest in producing a factual biographical account of the life of Jesus. They were interested in recapitulating the faith of Jesus. Why Jesus' faith and not that of some prophet? Ebeling coined the term *"Wortgeschehen"* (word event) and Fuchs *"Sprachereignis"* (language occurrence) to speak of the identity of Jesus. The Word engenders faith, so for Ebeling and Fuchs the important thing that came to expression in Jesus is faith. To believe in Jesus is to reenact the decision of faith that Jesus originally made. Their typical Lutheran reduction of theology to "Word" and "faith" was reflected in all their writings.[32]

The post-Bultmannian quest of the historical Jesus failed to connect with the high Christology of Paul and John that culminated in the Councils of Nicaea (A.D. 325) and Chalcedon (A.D. 451). For Ebeling the uniqueness of Jesus was that he was a witness to faith; he was the source and basis of faith. Ebeling thought that he could locate the beginnings of Christology in the "faith of Jesus." Bultmann countered this by saying that the "faith of Jesus" is an idea foreign to the New Testament.[33] Faith is not the new thing in the New Testament. Faith already existed in the Old

---

31. Bornkamm, *Jesus of Nazareth,* p. 21.

32. My doctoral mentor Paul Tillich once told me after returning from a visit to Switzerland, where he met Karl Barth for the first time after World War II and experienced a kind of reconciliation, that "all they are talking about now in German Protestant theology is 'Word' and 'faith.'" Cf. Ernst Fuchs, *Studies of the Historical Jesus,* tr. Andrew Scobie (London: SCM Press, 1964). Also, Gerhard Ebeling, *The Nature of Faith,* tr. Ronald Gregor Smith (Philadelphia: Muhlenberg Press, 1961). See also Ebeling's essays in *Word and Faith.*

33. Rudolf Bultmann, "The Primitive Christian Kerygma and the Historical Jesus," in *The Historical Jesus and the Kerygmatic Christ,* tr. Carl E. Braaten and Roy A. Harrisville (Nashville: Abingdon Press, 1964), p. 34.

Testament. The New Testament itself refers to Abraham as the "father of faith." Jesus is much more than a witness of faith. He was not the first to have faith in God. Jesus was not the first Christian; he was a Jew. The New Testament does not ask Christians to believe *as* Jesus did but to believe *in* him. Ebeling seemed to be echoing an idea of liberal Protestantism that Adolf von Harnack expressed in a popular book entitled *What Is Christianity?* Harnack wrote that the essence of Christianity lies in the religion *of* Jesus, not in the religion *about* Jesus. His portrayal of Jesus was completely unchristological. He wrote: "The gospel that Jesus preached has to do only with the Father and not with the Son. . . . It is perverse to make Christology the fundamental substance of the gospel."[34]

The results of the new quest were unimpressive from both historical and theological points of view. In attempting to construct a Christology from below, by starting with a stripped down Jesus, the new questers, Käsemann and the rest, ended up with a "low Christology."[35] The new quest was a movement internal to late twentieth-century German New Testament scholarship; it failed to have much influence in the English-speaking world of theology. The post-Bultmannian questers searched in vain for a kerygmatic point of departure in Jesus' faith, his preaching, his attitude or conduct, his self-understanding, his idea of grace, etc. None of those things is sufficient to account for the development of the Easter *kerygma* and the rise of early Christian belief.

The new questers tiptoed around the resurrection of Jesus as a real event of history. They did not advance the discussion beyond Bultmann's explanation of Easter as the rise of faith in the disciples. In the final analysis the Jesus of the new questers was just another version of the "so-called historical Jesus." The virtual exclusion of the resurrection of Jesus as a structural component of the revelation of God in Jesus Christ is the Achilles' heal of both the old and new quests of the historical Jesus. All these predominantly German questers shared the consensus that the event of the resurrection forms no part of the historical problem of the life of Jesus. Their efforts to establish a material connection between Jesus and the faith of the first Christians bypass the resurrection. Hans

---

34. Harnack, *What Is Christianity?* pp. 144, 184.

35. For a discussion of "high" and "low Christology" see chapter 4 below.

Conzelmann (1915-1989) formulated the issue before us in a crystal-clear way: "The resurrection was regarded by the primitive church as an event in space and time.... Of course, it did not reflect on the relation between the historical and supra-historical.... However, as soon as reflection sets in, ... it is evident that historical research cannot establish the facticity of the resurrection. It can only establish that men testified they had seen Jesus alive after his death." From that Conzelmann concludes that for us today it is clear "that the resurrection is not an historical event."[36] We will consider this question further in chapter three of this book, "Did Jesus Really Rise from the Dead?"

## The Third Quest of the Historical Jesus

Why did the Gospel writers refer to Jesus as the Christ, Messiah, Son of God, Son of Man, Lord, King, Master, Prophet, and Teacher? Why did the Fourth Gospel equate the Word with God in the first place (John 1:1) and then with Jesus in the second place (v. 14), so that the early Christians would go on to confess Jesus as "true God and true man"? Today, a renewal of the quest of the historical Jesus is in full swing. The "Jesus Seminar" is the most publicized example of what N. T. Wright has called the "Third Quest." The motivation of its leaders is not purely historical. They openly acknowledge that their aim is to create a new Christianity based on the real intentions of Jesus and on his authentic sayings and actions.[37] This new Christianity, they say, will not base itself on the secondhand Jesus of Peter, Paul, John, and the other apostles, who turned him into an object of faith, a Savior, placing him on a par with God.

Robert Funk (1926-2005) was the founder of the "Jesus Seminar." He, John Dominic Crossan, and Marcus Borg have been its most prolific and popular spokespersons. In his book *Honest to Jesus,* Funk states that

---

36. Hans Conzelmann, "Jesus Christus," in *Die Religion in Geschichte und Gegenwart* (3rd edition, Tübingen: J. C. B. Mohr, 1959), p. 650.

37. Robert W. Funk, Roy W. Hoover, and the Jesus Seminar, *The Five Gospels: The Search for the Authentic Words of Jesus* (New York: The Macmillan Co., 1993). Robert W. Funk and the Jesus Seminar, *The Acts of Jesus: The Search for the Authentic Deeds of Jesus* (San Francisco: HarperSanFrancisco, 1998).

the aim of the quest is to set Jesus free. Its purpose is to liberate Jesus from the scriptural and creedal and experiential prisons in which we have incarcerated him. . . . Just as the first believers did, we will have to start over again with a clean slate, with only the parables, aphorisms, parabolic acts, and deeds of Jesus as the basis on which to formulate a new version of the faith. . . . Jesus, rather than the Bible or the creeds, becomes the norm. . . . We can no longer rest our faith on the faith of Peter or the faith of Paul. I do not want my faith to be a second-hand faith. . . . I do not want to be misled by what Jesus' followers did. . . . Jesus himself should not be, must not be, the object of faith. That would be to repeat the idolatry of the first believers. . . . To be sure, it is not possible to foresee the complete shape of a reinvented Christianity.[38]

For Funk the chief sin of the early church was to worship Jesus as Lord.

John Dominic Crossan is the most erudite member of the "Jesus Seminar" and the author of numerous scholarly and popular books on Jesus.[39] Once a monk, he seems to be a modest and humble person, but as a historical scientist he boasts that he has acquired more accurate knowledge about Jesus than the Gospel writers, who based their reports on what eyewitnesses remembered about him. They said Jesus was crucified, that he died and was buried, and that he rose from the grave on the third day. Crossan says, yes, Jesus did die by crucifixion, but he was not buried, his body was most likely devoured by scavenging dogs, and he most assuredly was not raised bodily from the tomb. Jesus did not choose twelve disciples, the Last Supper never happened, and the events of Passion Week were all made up. How does he know so many things that nobody else knows? Very few scholars agree with his use of recently discovered gnostic and apocryphal Gospels as reliable new sources for reconstructing the life and message of Jesus, especially the *Gospel of Peter* and the *Gospel of Thomas*. I know of no scholars who agree with Crossan's identification of Jesus as a peasant Jewish Cynic.

38. Robert W. Funk, *Honest to Jesus* (San Francisco: HarperSanFrancisco, 1996), p. 300.

39. John Dominic Crossan, *The Historical Jesus: The Life of a Mediterranean Jewish Peasant* (San Francisco: HarperSanFrancisco, 1991); *Jesus: A Revolutionary Biography* (San Francisco: HarperSanFrancisco, 1994).

Enter Schweitzer and Kähler once again. Crossan's reconstructed image of Jesus is a transparent function of his own theological agenda. He portrays Jesus as a revolutionary whose vision of the kingdom of God was countercultural egalitarianism. Jesus was critical of all hierarchical power and oppressive structures, just like Crossan himself. Jesus practiced open table fellowship that was fully inclusive, especially of the outcasts and downtrodden. Jesus was non-patriarchal and non-institutional. Crossan appeals to Jesus to support his critique of the authoritarian hierarchicalism of his own Catholic tradition. Christianity went off the tracks from the start. It became an Easter faith. That was its first big mistake. The new vision of Christianity invented to suit modern sensibilities, one that Crossan and the "Jesus Seminar" are promoting, is vastly different from the ancient church with its biblical canon, liturgical cult, and dogmatic creed. Crossan has constructed yet another version of the "so-called historical Jesus" of no relevance or validity for Christian faith today. If any ordinary Christian layperson would ask me what to think about Crossan's Jesus, my answer would be "Who needs him?" The ideas he puts into Jesus' mouth would have been well received in the counterculture of the 1960s among the Hippies and Yippies.

Marcus Borg, a leading member of the "Jesus Seminar," devotes his search for the historical Jesus to the reformation of the Christian church.[40] He believes that most of what historic Christianity has confessed about Jesus in its creeds is simply untrue. Jesus was not a divine savior who died for the sins of the world. He was not raised from the dead. He did not preach the kingdom of God as a future eschatological reality whose coming will fundamentally transform the world. It is not important for us today to believe in Jesus, let alone worship him as God. What matters is to be like Jesus and to embody his countercultural vision. Only a radically new image of Jesus will make that possible.

Borg rejects the image of Jesus as an eschatological prophet that has dominated modern German New Testament scholarship; instead he portrays Jesus as a charismatic sage. Like Crossan, Borg discovers in Jesus certain values that he cherishes, such as freedom, equality, justice, and inclu-

---

40. Marcus Borg, *Conflict, Holiness, and Politics in the Teaching of Jesus* (New York: Edwin Mellen Press, 1984); *Jesus: A New Vision* (San Francisco: Harper & Row, 1988).

siveness. But why does anyone need Jesus to foster such beliefs? The *philosophes* of the French Enlightenment (Diderot, Voltaire, Rousseau) made these values the pillars of their social revolution without needing to refer to Jesus. Freedom, equality, and inclusiveness are the politically correct slogans most *au courant* at every meeting of today's academic professionals. Who can be against them? Yet in the New Testament Jesus' struggle is depicted as a dramatic victory over the powers of sin, death, and Satan. Borg's Jesus is totally different, with scarcely any basis in the eyewitness testimonies of the Gospels. He is just another version of the "so-called historical Jesus" who mirrors the author's social and cultural idealism.

Funk, Crossan, and Borg approach the New Testament with their own set of presuppositions. Nobody interprets anything without presuppositions. The problem is, these scholars claim to be purely objective and scientific with no axes to grind. They claim they have found the real Jesus, one who turns out to be unlike the Jesus remembered by the Gospel writers and unlike the Christ worshipped by Christians down through the centuries and across all cultures. The Jesus of the "Jesus Seminar" is a dead Palestinian Jew who was unlucky enough to get nabbed and nailed to a cross, due to a colossal misunderstanding — just a bad mix-up at city hall. Their Jesus is not the Word of God incarnate; he is not the Lamb of God who takes away the sin of the world; he was not resurrected to bring hope to a dying world. He was not the Messiah long-awaited by Old Testament Jews; he did not perform miracles; he did not teach the Lord's Prayer. Most of the parables and sayings were put in Jesus' mouth by others. He was not any of the things the early Christians said he was. In the end the "Jesus Seminar" portrays a Jesus not worth the bother.

The earliest believers gathered together after Easter to share what they remembered about Jesus; they believed he was present among them in the power of the Spirit. Since many of these reports come from eyewitness followers of Jesus, they are more credible than the speculative reconstructions of the "Jesus Seminar." Schweitzer and Kähler judged that the nineteenth-century biographers created pictures of Jesus after their own image. Their verdict is equally valid against the fantastic variety of images that contemporary scholars produce of Jesus. For S. G. F. Brandon, Jesus was a political revolutionary; for Hugh Schonfield, a messianic schemer; for Morton Smith, the founder of a secret society; for

C. F. Potter, a Qumran Essene; for Geza Vermes, a Galilean holy man; for Burton Mack, a wandering Cynic preacher; for John Dominic Crossan, a Mediterranean Jewish peasant Cynic; for Marcus Borg, a countercultural charismatic; for Elizabeth Schüssler Fiorenza, a feminist founder of an egalitarian community; for Barbara Thiering, a man who married Mary Magdalene, had two sons and a daughter, divorced Mary and married another woman, and died in his sixties; for A. N. Wilson, a Galilean sage who taught a simple form of Judaism. And, according to John Spong, Jesus was born of a woman who had been raped, and all the stuff about Christmas and Easter is merely later Christian midrash and mythology. Gerd Theissen has aptly stated, "The multiplicity of pictures of Jesus is reason to suspect that they are in reality self-portraits of their authors."[41] A person would have to be incredibly gullible to take them seriously.

## Critics of the "Jesus Seminar"

It is fair to say that leading New Testament scholars do not take the "Jesus Seminar" seriously. Its participants have evoked a vigorous outpouring of counter-criticism. The idiosyncratic use of gnostic and apocryphal sources and methodological guesswork has brought discredit to the sober use of historical criticism. The list of authors very critical of the "Jesus Seminar" and the Funk-Crossan-Borg axis is impressive and growing. These authors' contributions to the "Third Quest" now underway are much more consistent with the ways the Christian tradition has interpreted Jesus through the centuries.[42] Unlike the negative critics, these positive critics do not separate Jesus from historic Christianity or aim to undermine the authority of the New Testament canon. They are not trying to replace the Christ of faith with the Jesus of history. Their intentions are to be constructive. They accept as true and valid the high christological titles given to Jesus in the early church and the ancient creeds. The "they" I am referring to include the following authors: E. P.

41. Gerd Theissen and Annette Merz, *The Historical Jesus: A Comprehensive Guide,* tr. John Bowden (Minneapolis: Fortress Press, 1998), p. 13.

42. Cf. Jaroslav Pelikan, *Jesus through the Centuries* (New Haven: Yale University Press, 1985).

Sanders, N. T. Wright, James D. G. Dunn, Markus Bockmuehl, Ben Witherington III, Richard J. Bauckham, Craig A. Evans, Luke Timothy Johnson, John P. Meier, Joseph Ratzinger, and many others.[43]

Many of their writings about Jesus are edifying and illuminating, even on occasion devotionally inspiring and homiletically useful. Their interest in Jesus research is motivated by a deep commitment to the common faith of the Christian church. In comparing the works of the negative and the positive critical historians, we must be decidedly on the side of the latter. However, from a theological point of view we must still ask about the relevance of even the most positive reconstructions of the "historical Jesus." The results of historical research are never certain, always a matter of higher or lower degrees of probability. A historically reconstructed Jesus who *probably* understood himself as the Messiah or as the Son of Man, who *probably* said some or many of the things he was reported to have said, who *probably* performed some of the miracles attributed to him, but perhaps not all, who quite certainly was a preacher of the kingdom of God, but may or may not have had in mind a future eschatological kingdom — what is the relevance of such probability knowledge about the historical Jesus? A minimum of assured results, even if scholars could agree on such, cannot be made the basis of faith or establish the content of faith. The faith by which sinners are justified cannot be

43. E. P. Sanders, *Jesus and Judaism* (Philadelphia: Fortress Press, 1985); N. T. Wright, *Jesus and the Victory of God* (Minneapolis: Fortress Press, 1996); *Who Was Jesus?* (Grand Rapids: Eerdmans Publishing Co., 1992); James D. G. Dunn, *The Evidence for Jesus* (Philadelphia: Westminster Press, 1985); *Jesus Remembered* (Grand Rapids: Eerdmans Publishing Co., 2003); *A New Perspective on Jesus: What the Quest for the Historical Jesus Missed* (Grand Rapids: Baker Academic, 2005); *Jesus, Paul, and the Gospels* (Grand Rapids: Eerdmans, 2011); Markus Bockmuehl, *This Jesus: Martyr, Lord, Messiah* (Edinburgh: T. & T. Clark, 1994); *The Cambridge Companion to Jesus* (Cambridge University Press, 2001); Ben Witherington III, *The Christology of Jesus* (Minneapolis: Fortress Press, 1990); *The Jesus Quest: The Third Search for the Jew of Nazareth* (Downers Grove, Ill.: InterVarsity Press, 1995); Richard J. Bauckham, *Jesus and the Eyewitnesses: The Gospels as Eyewitness Testimony* (Grand Rapids: Wm B. Eerdmans Publishing Co., 2006); Craig A. Evans, *Fabricating Jesus: How Modern Scholars Distort the Gospels* (Downers Grove, Ill.: InterVarsity Press, 2006); Luke Timothy Johnson, *The Real Jesus: The Misguided Quest for the Historical Jesus and the Truth of the Traditional Gospels* (San Francisco: HarperSanFrancisco, 1996); John P. Meier, *A Marginal Jew: Rethinking the Historical Jesus* (New York: Doubleday, 1991); Pope Benedict XVI, *Jesus of Nazareth*, tr. Adrian J. Walker (New York: Doubleday, 2007).

made dependent on the results of historical research, even if they appear to be a consensus among positive critics.

If Christian scholars believe they must join the quest for the historical Jesus, whether in obedience to the scientific *eros* or as an expression of their belief in the humanity of Christ, they should not claim for its results finality of meaning for faith and doctrine. Yet some scholars persist in maintaining the theological necessity of the quest. Decades ago James Robinson expressed the opinion still held by many: "The theological necessity of the new quest resides in the situation in which we find ourselves today, committed to a *kerygma* which locates its saving event in a historical person to whom we have a second avenue of access because of the rise of scientific historiography since the Enlightenment. . . . These two avenues of access to the same person create a situation which has not existed in the Church since the time of those original disciples who had both their Easter faith and their memory of Jesus."[44]

Such pseudo-scientific hubris is appalling. James Robinson thereby ascribes to himself and his fellow questers the role of the original apostles. If we truly have a second means of access to the real Jesus in addition to the apostolic preaching of Jesus as the Christ recorded in the Gospels, then the newly constructed historico-scientific synopsis of the authentic words and deeds of Jesus would give us what Ernst Renan (1823-1892) called for, a "Fifth Gospel." This new Gospel would supposedly be more reliable than the four Gospels; it would have met the modern test of scientific historiography. If that is the case, as the "Jesus Seminar" claims it to be, then we would have what it takes to launch a new Christianity in the name of Jesus!

Does the modern historian who is also a Christian believer wish to assume the function of an apostle, a mediator of a saving existential encounter with Jesus Christ? The mere suggestion is absurd on its face. To meet Jesus again, now for the second time by way of scientific historiography and no longer merely by means of the apostolic witness, ordinary Christians presumably need to be instructed by critical historians as to which of the words and deeds attributed to Jesus in the Gospels are gen-

---

44. James Robinson, "The New Quest of the Historical Jesus," *Theology Today* 15 (1958-59): 192-93.

uine. But which ones? No consensus exists whatsoever among biblical scholars on any significant matter. Nor can they appeal to a higher authority, to what Kähler called a "papacy of higher learning."

The old and new quests of the historical Jesus were rejected not only by systematic theologians like Karl Barth and Paul Tillich, but by the self-correcting process of historical-critical scholarship. The same thing is now occurring with respect to the so-called "Third Quest." No dogmatician needs to enter the fray: the historians refute each other by contesting the evidences they adduce to support their novel hypotheses. There is nothing unusual about this: the scientific method is an endless process of trial and error. Methodologically the quest for the historical Jesus will continue to peel away the layers of the Gospel tradition to reach an oral period that transmits the *ipsissima verba et acta*[45] of Jesus. Some professional historians make a good living doing that, writing popular books and bestsellers. A number of them do so to drive a wedge between Jesus and the church, while others seem to do so in the mistaken belief that the pursuit of the quest is necessary for Christian faith and theology. They are mistaken to think that questions of faith must be held in limbo until all questions of fact are resolved. The oscillations of scientific inquiry never come to rest. The "assured results" of today are repudiated as fictions of the imagination tomorrow. The old quest from Reimarus to Wrede was roundly rejected by the new quest of Käsemann and Bornkamm, and the "Third Quest" from Borg to Wright rejects as meretricious both of the two previous ones. The conclusion seems irresistible: the real Jesus is not and never can be the end-product of a scholarly quest. He is the living risen Christ remembered first by eyewitnesses and then transmitted to following generations through Spirit-inspired manuscripts. We have the eyewitness testimonies in the canonical manuscripts, and if we do not meet the real Jesus there, we will not meet him at all.

The always disputable results of the old and new quests of the historical Jesus cannot provide the basis and content of faith. This is not to reject historical criticism as a method to apply in biblical interpretation. The point is, rather, that the always fluctuating results of biblical criticism are powerless to mediate the living biblical Christ of faith, who is al-

---

45. "The very words and acts themselves."

ways at the same time the crucified and risen earthly Jesus. With respect to faith in Christ the most sophisticated theologian is in no better or worse a position than the simple Christian. A plain reading of Scripture mediates a living impression of the "whole Christ of the whole Bible" without any need to appeal to dogmatic or historical authorities. An essential dependence of faith upon the results of historical research would force faith to rely on the erudition of learned professors. Faith that must rest on a prior belief in authority is not the kind of faith that the apostle Paul spoke of when he said that a person is justified by God through faith in Jesus Christ (Rom. 3:22).

## Questions for Discussion

1. What documentary sources do you think give us the most reliable knowledge about Jesus of Nazareth?

2. What would you say to a person who doubted whether Jesus really existed?

3. How important is it to you that historians continue the search for the historical Jesus?

4. Some translations of the New Testament print everything Jesus said in red letters. The "Jesus Seminar" offers a different color scheme. Jesus' sayings are printed in red, pink, gray, and black. Red means that Jesus undoubtedly said it, pink that he probably said something like it, gray that he did not say it but the idea was somewhat like his, and black that he surely did not say it. What sense does this make to your picture of Jesus?

5. Do you think the results of the quest for the historical Jesus are important for the Christian faith? If so, in what way? If not, what is the point of the scholarly search for the real Jesus of history?

6. Do you think saving faith is dependent on the results of historical inquiry, inasmuch as they are always a matter of a higher or lower degree of probability?

7. The questers say that the Gospel of John is not historically reliable, as compared to the Gospels of Matthew, Mark, and Luke. Do you think that diminishes John's value as a text for preaching the gospel of Christ? Why or why not?

# II

# How Do Christians Come to Believe in Jesus?

*I believe that by my own reason or strength I cannot believe in Jesus Christ, my Lord, or come to him. But the Holy Spirit has called me through the Gospel, enlightened me with his gifts, and sanctified and preserved me in true faith, just as he calls, gather, enlightens, and sanctifies the whole Christian church on earth and preserves it in union with Jesus Christ in the one true faith.*

Martin Luther, *Small Catechism*, Article III

In our first chapter we dealt with the question, "What can we know about Jesus of Nazareth?" Part of our answer was to reject the popular notion in academic circles that we gain reliable access to the real Jesus of history only by searching behind the plain texts of the Gospels. After more than two hundred years of historical research no consensus has emerged among scholars on the personal identity and religious significance of Jesus. The question Jesus himself put to his disciples on the way to Caesarea Philippi, "Who do people say that I am?" (Mark 8:27; Luke 9:18) evoked different answers in his lifetime. Some said Jesus was John the Baptist *redivivus,* others that he was one of the ancient prophets, such as Elijah, come back to life. Today's scholars have added a plethora of answers to the question of Jesus' identity: he is a sage, a Cynic, a prophet, a revolutionary, a visionary, a charismatic, a spirit person, a holy man, a magician, an Essene, an apocalyptist. Why is it so difficult for many of today's scholars to accept Peter's answer to Jesus' question, "You are the Messiah" (Mark 8:29)? Even the demoniacs in the country of the Gadarenes hailed Jesus as the "Son of God" (Matt. 8:28-29). And the centurion at the cross cried out, "Truly this man was God's Son!" (Matt. 15:39) All the evangelists — Matthew, Mark, Luke, and John — agreed on this: Jesus is the Messiah of God, the Son of God.

How do we today come to know who Jesus really is? Marcus J. Borg is one of the leading scholars of the "Jesus Seminar." In his popular book, *Meeting Jesus Again for the First Time,* he tells of how he came to reject his childhood image of Jesus as the divinely begotten Son of God who died for the sins of the world. Borg briefly attended Union Seminary in New York and received a Master's degree from Oxford University in England. He claims that in the course of his studies he learned that the Gospels tell us not who Jesus really was but only what the first generations of Christians believed about him. He learned that the historical Jesus behind the Gospels is vastly different from the Jesus Christ of the New Testament and the Christian community. The Gospels picture Jesus the way he was seen after Easter. This is the "post-Easter Jesus" in Borg's terminology,[1] the Christ of faith at the center of the worshipping community. Borg is more interested in the "pre-Easter Jesus," who supposedly is utterly different from the post-Easter Jesus. Borg's pre-Easter Jesus was a "spirit person, one of those figures in human history with an experiential awareness of the reality of God."[2] Jesus was other things as well: a teacher of wisdom, a social prophet, and a founder of a renewal movement within Judaism.

Borg draws the following conclusions from his reconstructed image of Jesus: the pre-Easter Jesus was not God and was not unique. He was one among many religious personalities who have experienced God as a numinous reality such as Buddha, Muhammad, or Lao-tsu. This is what Borg understands, now that he is an adult and a scholar. He has put away childish things, like believing in Jesus as the Gospels portray him and as the church has taught in its creeds and liturgies.[3]

1. Marcus J. Borg, *Meeting Jesus Again for the First Time* (San Francisco: HarperSanFrancisco, 1994), p. 15.

2. Borg, *Meeting Jesus,* p. 30.

3. Borg, *Meeting Jesus,* p. 136.

Borg's quest for the "pre-Easter Jesus" is not fundamentally different from the old quest of the historical Jesus. The criticisms of Kähler and Schweitzer still apply. Borg has fabricated an image of Jesus and substituted it for the picture of Jesus as the Christ in the Gospels. His idea of what it means to be a Christian is similar to Harnack's. The religion *about* Jesus is replaced by the religion *of* Jesus. Borg's image of Jesus "shifts the focus of the Christian life from believing in Jesus or believing in God to being in relationship to the same Spirit that Jesus knew."[4] To put the matter differently, Borg thinks that being a Christian is to emulate Jesus' relationship to the Spirit rather than to *believe in* Jesus as the Christ of God. For Borg the former is an adult perspective, the latter is childish.

The Spirit that Marcus Borg has in mind is not the Spirit that Martin Luther refers to in his explanation of the third article of the Apostles' Creed:

> As the Father is called Creator and the Son is called Redeemer, so on account of his work the Holy Spirit must be called Sanctifier, the One who makes holy. . . . He leads us into his holy community, placing us upon the bosom of the church, where he preaches to us and brings us to Christ. Neither you nor I could ever know anything of Christ, or believe in him and take him as our Lord, unless these were first offered to us and bestowed on our hearts through the preaching of the Gospel by the Holy Spirit.[5]

We have before us two completely different visions of how we meet Jesus today, Borg's and Luther's. For Borg and the "Jesus Seminar" in general the only credible way to meet Jesus today is to search and deliver him from obscurity behind the Gospel texts. For Luther and the mainstream of the Christian tradition the only way to meet Jesus is through the preaching of the Word, mediated by the sacred Scriptures, within the community of faith, and empowered by the Holy Spirit. The former oc-

---

4. Borg, *Meeting Jesus*, p. 39.

5. Martin Luther, "The Large Catechism," in *The Book of Concord*, tr. and ed. Theodore G. Tappert (Philadelphia: Fortress Press, 1959), p. 415.

curs by a work that only scholars can perform; the latter is the way of faith engendered solely as a work of the Holy Spirit by means of the word of apostolic preaching. The real Jesus who reveals God to us remains hidden to all those who do not come to him through a personal and living faith. Yes, it is a matter of faith born of the Spirit accessible to any ordinary layperson and not a work of the intellect that only a few highly skilled practitioners of historical scholarship can perform. This is the epistemological significance of the doctrine of justification by faith, the hallmark of a theology of salvation that both Protestants and Catholics have in common.[6] Genuine Christian knowledge presupposes a living faith in God who reveals himself in Jesus as the Christ, a knowledge unmediated by the results of the modern quest for the historical Jesus behind the Gospels. A reconstructed image of the historical Jesus separated from the framing of his picture as the Christ of God in the Gospels is not only a dubious historico-scientific enterprise, but is also of no apologetic value or theological significance. Not the first, nor the second, nor the third quest of the historical Jesus gives faith the means of access to the saving revelation of God in Jesus Christ.

## Faith and Historical Reason

Apart from faith there can be no knowledge of God's self-revelation in the person of Jesus as the Christ. The "Jesus Seminar" folks who claim to know who Jesus was apart from his filial relation to God his Father and apart from his identity as the Messiah of Israel are pursuing a faith-less project. They apply the tools of historical criticism by reason alone, apart from faith and the beliefs and doctrines of the Christian community. Since they presuppose that Jesus is not more than a man, every statement in the Gospels that frames the identity and meaning of Jesus in supra-historical symbols is dismissed as mythological in the pejorative sense of that term, as misleading and untrue. Their historical Jesus is not

6. On October 31, 1999, Catholics and Lutherans signed the "Joint Declaration on the Doctrine of Justification," thus burying the hatchet on their chief point of difference since the sixteenth century, though there are theologians on both sides who continue to dispute the theological accuracy of the agreement.

more than a man, a belief that runs counter to everything believed about him from the first generation of Christians to the present time. Such a negative judgment does not mean that the modern methods of historical reason are of no value to Christian theology. The question is: In which context of understanding are they best applied? N. T. Wright has written: "Among other beliefs, I hold more firmly than ever to the conviction that serious study of Jesus and the gospels is best done within the context of the worshipping community."[7]

The modern methods of historical criticism used in the study of the Bible are here to stay. We have no interest in turning back the clock to a pre-critical period of biblical theology. However, the assumption of some scholars that historical criticism is a neutral science is a self-deception. Secular scholars approach the Bible with their own set of prior commitments, no less than do biblical scholars who openly acknowledge their ecclesial context of inquiry. In the latter case, it should be similarly not surprising, nor denied, that theologians of the church bring their own faith perspectives to bear on their historical research. After all, the Bible is the book of the church; through a lengthy process of selection and discernment the church finally created the canon.

A faith perspective is fully compatible with a robust use of reason in historical research. In fact, there is no way to pursue any kind of inquiry apart from reason. Christian faith is not non-rational. Faith is a self-surrendering commitment of the whole person to the transcendent reality of God. The whole person is inclusive of intellect, will, and trust. In old scholastic terms, faith is not mere feeling and emotion; it comprises *notitia* (intellectual knowledge), *assensus* (assent of the will), and *fiducia* (heartfelt trust).[8] An existential response to the historical revelation of God in Jesus of Nazareth involves both reason and faith. Reason needs faith as the dynamic of its vision. Apart from faith reason is blind, and apart from reason faith is empty, to paraphrase one of Immanuel Kant's (1724-1804) famous formulas. *What* reason sees is seen by reason, but

---

7. N. T. Wright, *Who Was Jesus?* (Grand Rapids: Wm. B. Eerdmans Publishing Co., 1992), p. ix.

8. Cf. Heinrich Schmid, *The Doctrinal Theology of the Evangelical Lutheran Church,* rev. and tr. by Charles A. Hay and Henry E. Jacobs (Minneapolis: Augsburg Publishing House, 1899), pp. 410-11.

*that* reason sees what it sees is made possible by faith. Apart from what Søren Kierkegaard called "infinite personal passionate interest," the truth and reality of God's appearance in Jesus of Nazareth remain hidden and undisclosed to secular reason operating within its own limits.

A purely fideistic[9] approach to the truth of God's revelation in Jesus Christ is as one-sided as a purely rationalistic one. The folly of fideism is to base faith on faith, generating the content of faith out of its own subjectivity, never mind the objective facts. This reminds one of the preacher who, coming to a weak point in his discourse, wrote in the margin of his sermon notes, "shout loudly." When the truth claims of faith are placed beyond the reach of reason, that frees faith to postulate whatever is subjectively satisfying. The fatal consequence of fideism is that it gives rise to the impression that its statements are arbitrary and need not be taken seriously outside the circle of faith. When faith generates its own beliefs with no check on the evidence within reason's grasp, what is to distinguish such faith from superstition or illusion?

Christian theology cannot move forward on two separated tracks, faith and reason. It is not the case that autonomous reason establishes the facts and that faith adds an arbitrary interpretation. A split between reason and faith or between facts and interpretations leads to noetic schizophrenia. When reason's role is removed from the act of faith, there is nothing to keep faith from self-delusion. The confession that Jesus is the Christ is a combination of a fact of history and an interpretation of faith, but they stand and fall together. There are no facts without interpretations. Historical knowledge and faith knowledge are unified in the act of confessing Jesus as the Christ of God.


## The Testimony of the Holy Spirit

Wright's claim that the study of Jesus and the Gospels is best done within the context of the worshipping community entails the belief that Jesus as a past historical figure is a living presence in the present time. The

9. Fideism is a theory of knowledge that maintains that faith is sufficient of itself apart from reason to discover religious truth.

knowledge that Jesus is not dead but alive depends on believing participation in the sacramental practices of the Christian community. It is an observable fact that scholars who study the Bible within the context of the believing community reach vastly different results than those who, for whatever reasons, do not share the faith and teachings of the Christian church. What does this prove? Only that faith makes a difference.

The study of Jesus apart from faith will at best view him as a moral example or religious genius of some kind. The result will be a Jesusology, treating Jesus perhaps as an object of hero worship. The church's Christology is something else. Its task is to account for the central place of Jesus as the Christ in the life and worship of the church. Anthropolatry is a sin, the kind of worship of Jesus as a mere man that often goes on in the kind of liberal Protestantism that denies the truth of God incarnate, the Nicene confession that Jesus is "very God of very God." The judgment of faith that the person of Jesus is homogeneous with God, that is, "of one substance with the Father," is not a self-induced performance of the human intellect and will.

Faith is made possible by the witness of the Holy Spirit, a gift of grace alone. Faith's acceptance of the biblical portrayal of the identity and meaning of Jesus Christ is brought about by the inspiration of the Holy Spirit. In reading and studying the same book that conveys the revelation of God in Jesus of Nazareth, why do some believe and others do not? It is an age-old mystery that the apostle Paul explained with his statement that "the god of this world has blinded the minds of the unbelievers, to keep them from seeing the light of the gospel of the glory of Christ, who is the image of God" (2 Cor. 4:4). A more positively worded insight was given by John the evangelist: "When the Spirit of truth comes, he will guide you into all the truth; for he will not speak on his own, but he will speak whatever he hears, and he will declare to you the things that are to come. He will glorify me, because he will take what is mine and declare it to you" (John 16:13-14). The ancient fathers and church reformers also taught that people are brought to faith in Jesus as the Christ through the *"testimonium Spiritus Sancti internum."*[10] John Calvin (1509-1564) put it succinctly:

10. "Internal testimony of the Holy Spirit."

The testimony of the Spirit is superior to reason. For as God alone can properly bear witness to his own words, so these words will not obtain full credit in the hearts of men, until they are sealed by the inward testimony of the Spirit. The same Spirit who speaks by the mouth of the prophets must penetrate our hearts in order to convince us that they faithfully delivered the message with which they were divinely entrusted.[11]

The appeal of faith to the witness of the Holy Spirit does not call for a *sacrificium intellectus*[12] on the altar of an authoritarian belief system. Neither the old Protestant doctrine of a verbally inerrant Bible nor the modern Roman Catholic dogma of papal infallibility is needed to secure the access of faith to the revelation of God in Jesus Christ.

Søren Kierkegaard asked the question, "How do we today become contemporary with Christ?" The relationship of personal faith to the living Christ of the Bible is mediated by the Holy Spirit. Therefore, it is not accurate to say that faith alone bridges the gap between the past and the present and between time and eternity. Faith is not that athletic; apart from the empowerment of the Holy Spirit it is impotent. Faith is our "yes" to the promise of the presence of Christ who enters our life by the work of the Holy Spirit. Christ becomes our contemporary as a powerful redeeming presence by the mediation of the Holy Spirit. The Spirit applies the benefits of the death and resurrection of Jesus to a sinful and dying human race. This donation of the Spirit does not happen as a reward for believing certain unbelievable things about God, Jesus, or the Bible. That is a mistaken idea of faith. It is the work of the Holy Spirit to actualize the presence of the living Christ and thereby convince a sinner to surrender his or her life to Jesus Christ through acts of repentance and faith. The real Jesus is the living Christ of faith, not the "historical Jesus" of the various quests that produce a wild variety of probable or improbable facts about a man called "Jesus." Historical critical research does not bring about an existential encounter with Jesus, as Marcus Borg claims. By it-

11. John Calvin, *Institutes of the Christian Religion*, tr. Henry Beveridge (Edinburgh: T. & T. Clark, 1879), I, p. 72.

12. "Sacrifice of the intellect."

self historical reason cannot realize the redeeming presence of the living Jesus; only the illuminating work of the Holy Spirit can make the scales fall from the eyes, a kind of reenactment of Paul's experience in Damascus (Acts 9:18).

## The Living Christ in the Preaching of the Church

The Holy Spirit of God the Father and the Lord Jesus Christ does not work directly within human experience apart from certain means that he has chosen. He works through the means of grace, through the audible words of preaching, and the visible words of the sacraments. Both the audible and visible words communicate the one Word of God who is Jesus Christ. What we say here in focusing on the preaching of the Word is also true *mutatis mutandis* with respect to all the communicative practices of the church. The risen Jesus becomes a reality in the experience of faith by means of the living voice of the gospel (the *viva vox evangelii*). This does not happen automatically whenever preachers open their mouths. Real hearing of the Word is under the Spirit's control; it happens where and when it pleases the Spirit of God.[13] Two brothers can hear the same message; one is moved to tears of repentance and faith, and the other turns a deaf ear to so much gobbledygook. This is the "Cain and Abel" phenomenon in human experience and history impenetrable to the smartest psychologists.

The Holy Spirit can cause a human word to become the Word of God and create the conviction of faith that Christ is really present to redeem from guilt and sin. Contemporary images of Jesus as an extraordinary human figure reconstructed by the Jesus critics have no power to do anything except to be a topic of endless debate in the guild of biblical scholars. Robert Funk founded the "Jesus Seminar" to leverage his call for a new religion in Jesus' name. Like the old attempts to invent a new Christianity modeled on the religion and ethics of Jesus, it has already petered out because it lacked the power of the Spirit to save and to serve. It was just an academic yo-yo.

---

13. *Ubi et quando deus vult.*

The preaching of Christ that awakens faith happens within the context of the church and by its ministries. Outside the church there is no gospel of salvation that draws its spiritual power from the death and resurrection of Jesus.[14] Christ-centered preaching takes place only within the community of those who confess Jesus as Lord and Savior. This is not to deny that there are other kinds of interest in Jesus of Nazareth besides that of the modern Jesus scholars who aim to substitute their own fabricated images for the biblical framing of the story of Jesus attested by the church for millennia. While there are still some people who deny the existence of Jesus, all the major religions acknowledge him as a world-historical figure of extraordinary stature. For Christians Jesus is the Lord and Liberator of life, the Son of God and Savior of humankind. For people of other religions Jesus is quite readily revered as a person of spiritual and moral strength. Jews and Muslims and Hindus and Buddhists can accept Jesus as one of the prophets, revealers, avatars, or such.

In the dialogue of the world religions, Christians should start the conversation at whatever level of interest persons of other religious persuasions express in Jesus, but then go on to witness to their belief that Jesus is God's gift of salvation, not for Christians alone, but for the whole world that God loves. Today Jews are reclaiming Jesus as one of their own. Muslims look to the Qur'an to learn its teachings about Jesus as a prophet and messenger of Allah. Hindus can incorporate Jesus into their pantheon of divine figures, along with Krishna, Rama, Isvara, and Purusha. Buddhists compare the story of Jesus favorably with their story of Gautama, the enlightened one, who became a poor wandering preacher and like Jesus entered into conflict with the religious authorities. Christian theologians involved in inter-religious dialogues are not expected to interject the latest hypotheses of the Jesus critics but to give witness to what they believe on the basis of their sacred Scriptures. And they should expect no less from their partners in dialogue. The problem for the Christian mission is that alien manifestations of interest in Jesus of Nazareth may inoculate people against the church's witness to the canonical Christ. If they believe they already know who Jesus is, why should they listen to the church?

---

14. This I take to be the kernel of truth in St. Cyprian's formula, *"Extra ecclesiam nulla salus."*

The Holy Spirit writes his autobiography throughout the course of church history. The church is God's chosen instrument and sacrament of what his Holy Spirit is doing in the world. Working in and through the church, the Holy Spirit is the mediator between the word of witness to Christ in the Bible and the hearing of the Word in the context of the church today. An individual cannot have a personal relationship with Jesus apart from the communion of saints, from whose witness a person's faith is engendered. The Gospel of John quotes Jesus as saying that "when the Spirit of truth comes . . . he will not speak on his own, but will speak whatever he hears. . . . He will take what is mine and declare it to you" (16:34). This is doubly true of the church. She has nothing of her own to give to the world. She can only pass on what she has received from Christ through the Spirit who dwells within. The Spirit empowers the church to serve and obey the living Christ as the Savior of the world and humanity.

The factors of faith, reason, Spirit, and Scripture that we have discussed are links in a hermeneutical chain that connects the living risen Christ to faithful preaching of the gospel by the church today. This hermeneutical chain is important for two reasons: 1) it protects the church from the temptation of using its beliefs and doctrines to secure its own self-aggrandizing power and privilege in the world, and 2) it keeps the church vigilant against the perennial threat of conforming its message to current cultural trends. The post-Constantinian church often succumbed to the first temptation, whereas post-Reformation Protestantism has often syncretized its message with the cultural isms of the day. That happened to the churches in Germany under Hitler when they melded the Christian message with Hitler's Nazi ideology. It is happening to the churches today, both on the left and on the right, when the neo-gnostic culture of American religion is accomplishing a massive invasion of the pulpits, pews, and policies of the denominations. The hermeneutical chain that links the church to its normative foundation in the canonical Scriptures, interpreted by the creedal and moral traditions of historic Christianity, is broken in all the liberal denominations of American Protestantism. The mainline churches are all in decline as they no longer uphold the core beliefs of the orthodox Christian tradition.

Suspicion is widespread in academia that linking use of the historical-critical method to the church and its confession of faith will skew the entire enterprise. Many users of the method do not accept N. T. Wright's opinion that critical historical study of the Bible is best carried on within the context of the worshipping community. To introduce the idea of God into a purely scientific enterprise is supposedly both irrelevant and distorting because it predetermines or at least compromises the results in advance of the empirical findings. With regard to our question of how we today can come to know who the real Jesus is, apart from waiting for the latest results of the "Jesus Seminar" or some other scholars, how may we be sure that the Christ of the church is not as much of a fabrication as the "historical Jesus" of Funk, Crossan, or Borg? If it is true, as I believe it is, that the church as the worshipping community is the essential context for the Spirit's work of actualizing the presence of Jesus Christ through the proclamation of the gospel, how is the Christ of the church the Lord of the church? Faith needs to know that Christ is not a mythic projection of a longing for salvation from this finite and evil world. The "Christ-myth" hypothesis of David F. Strauss (1808-1874) will always remain as a sober reminder of faith's need to know that Jesus is not only the Christ but also the Lord of the church, and not the other way around.

What makes the church Christian is its acceptance of Jesus as the Christ. As there is no church without Christ, there is no knowledge of Jesus as the Christ apart from the church. No historical scientific quest can reach the conclusion that Jesus is the Christ. Jesus cannot be known to be the Christ apart from the preaching and confession of the worshipping community. Any other kind of interest or knowledge regarding Jesus is to know him *kata sarka*,[15] as a mere man, and not as the One whom the Gospels make known to us, the Christ of the church. To say that "there is no Christ apart from the church and no church apart from Christ"[16] must be understood strictly as a correlation in the order of knowledge *(ordo cognoscendi),* and not in the order of being *(ordo essendi).* Participation in the life of the church is therefore essential to the knowledge of Jesus as the Christ, but not to his being. The reality of

---

15. *Kata sarka* means "according to the flesh" and appears in 2 Cor. 5:16.

16. This is one of the propositions in a preliminary draft of theological theses that Paul Tillich wrote and circulated among his students in preparation for writing his *Systematic Theology.*

Christ is prior to the church as the foundation is prior to the house which it supports.

The attempt of modern Protestantism to "get back to Jesus" to gain leverage against the self-sufficiency of a triumphalist orthodoxy is understandable but misguided. It is understandable as a reaction to Protestant Orthodoxy, which gave the impression that Christians believe in Christ because they believe in the Bible, and that they believe in the Bible because it is true, inerrant, and infallible. The authority of the Bible was maximalized to counter the growing authority of the Pope in Roman Catholicism. In Roman Catholic apologetics the authority of the magisterium guaranteed the authority of church tradition and the Bible. But the approach of modern Protestantism was also misguided because it fell from the frying pan of an objectivist system of authority into the fire of a subjectivism of historical relativism. If the temptation of Protestant fundamentalism is to elevate the Bible above Christ, the temptation of Roman Catholicism is to elevate the church above Christ. Both approaches diminish the Lordship of Christ and under-represent the church's relation of radical dependence and subservience to the Christ it confesses as Lord and Savior.

## The Whole Christ of the Whole Bible

The real Jesus is the living Word preached by the church and as such not an abstract schema into which each age pours its own social ideals and moral principles. That was precisely the accusation that Albert Schweitzer leveled against the nineteenth-century biographers of Jesus and, as we have shown, the same verdict applies to the Jesus scholars who are remaking the image of Jesus after their own kind. It is true, of course, that the picture of Jesus has changed from time to time. In his book *Jesus through the Centuries*,[17] Jaroslav Pelikan (1923-2006) depicts the many faces of Jesus that appear in church history, from the eschatological Messiah in the Pauline communities, to the incarnate Logos in

---

17. Jaroslav Pelikan, *Jesus through the Centuries* (New Haven: Yale University Press, 1999).

Hellenistic Christianity, to the Pantocrator in Byzantine iconography, to the model of asceticism in medieval monasticism, to the bridegroom of the soul in mystical spirituality, to the enlightened social reformer in liberal Protestantism, to name just a few. Schweitzer wrote the epitaph of this phenomenon: "Each successive epoch of theology found its own thoughts in Jesus; that was, indeed, the only way in which it could make him live." This is not only true but also to the good. These historic movements drew their inspiration from something given in the Gospels' portrayal of Jesus, some symbol or story that overwhelmed them in their reading of the canonical texts. That is a far cry from what Schweitzer said about the Jesus questers: "Each individual created him (Jesus) in accordance with his own character. There is no historical task which so reveals a man's true self as the writing of a life of Jesus."[18]

Our theological criticism of the modern search for the historical Jesus would be too one-sided if it overlooked the fact that the movement has renewed the interest of Christian faith and preaching in taking more seriously the true and full humanity of Jesus Christ. Classical theology weighted its treatment of Jesus Christ on the side of his divinity, drawing mostly from the New Testament writings of Paul and John. The pendulum in modern theology has swung to the side of seeing Jesus as a real human being, focusing more on the Synoptic Gospels of Matthew, Mark, and Luke. But the confession of faith that Jesus was fully human is not a modern insight of historical scholarship; it was unqualifiedly affirmed by the anti-gnostic fathers Irenaeus, Hippolytus, and Tertullian. Nevertheless, nothing is gained for the Christian faith and life by playing the picture of Jesus as a human being in the Gospels, in support of a "low Christology," off against the belief in Jesus as the Son of God in John and the Epistles of Paul as warrant for a "high Christology." Taking either part of the New Testament at the expense of the other seriously obscures and threatens the church's commitment to "the whole Christ of the whole Bible." Christology must always overcome the antithesis between the Scylla of an ebionism, stressing the humanity of Jesus at the expense of his divinity, and the Charybdis of a docetism, stressing his divinity at the expense of his humanity. Jesus

18. Albert Schweitzer, *The Quest of the Historical Jesus*, p. 4.

Christ is both truly divine and truly human, one person in two natures (so the Council of Chalcedon, A.D. 451).

The New Testament is the record of the apostolic witness and preaching that brings the whole biblical Christ into the total life and worship of the church. Our contemporary access to the living Christ Jesus is mediated primarily through the apostolic testimonies. The claim of historical critics to possess new knowledge of Jesus from sources other than the canonical books of the New Testament contributes nothing to the gospel of salvation preached by the church. This does not mean that an individual Christian first comes to know Jesus through his or her own reading of the Bible. In most cases the ordinary Christian meets Jesus first through the lively communication of the Word in family settings and assemblies of worship. Whatever the particular circumstances, an individual is assured by the church that its witness to Jesus as the Christ is ultimately resourced and normed by the Bible and is not a product of its own creative imagination. A simple Christian has access to the biblical Christ in the same way as a learned theologian, since faith is not dependent on how much knowledge a person may have about the Bible and the Christian tradition.

The preaching of the church today awakens faith in Christ to the extent that it remains faithful to the apostolic picture of Jesus as the Christ in the Bible. This insight implies that a novel image of Jesus constructed by secular historians today lies outside the circle of Christian faith and theology. The result of deconstructing the Gospels' testimonies to Jesus as the Christ, Lord, and Redeemer is unavoidably a disfiguration that the Christian community can only reject as heresy, as the church fathers did with the presentations of Jesus in the gnostic Gospels and as the Confessing Church did with the Aryan Jesus of the German Christians under Nazism. What gives rise to heresy in the church is any treatment of Jesus that betrays and distorts the New Testament message in a fundamental way.

Why should the Bible be given such an irreplaceable position of privilege in the faith and theology of the Christian church? Why not accept as equally valid extra-canonical Gospels? Part of the answer is that they have not been used by the Holy Spirit to create the faith of those who confess Jesus as the Christ of God. They have not been the source of the preaching that established the church and shaped its faith and teachings through the centuries until today. They have not contributed to the missionary planting of the church on all continents and to the movements of evangelical reform and revival that have grown the church. The extracanonical sources that refer to Jesus, some of them Roman, Jewish, and gnostic, may be of historical interest, but they do not provide another means of access to the living Christ who encounters us in the church's transmission of the gospel derived from the witness and preaching of the apostles. Disciples of Jesus, who have the experience of coming to faith in him as the very Christ who appears through the medium of the biblical witnesses, will not look for another.

The Old Testament is just as much as the New Testament an essential part of the totality of the biblical revelation of God in Jesus Christ. Martin Luther said this about the Old Testament: "Here you will find the swaddling clothes and the manger in which Christ lies, and to which the angel points the shepherds (Luke 2:12). Simple and lowly are these swaddling clothes, but clear is the treasure, Christ, who lies in them."[19] Marcion (ca. 85-160) and the Christian gnostics, old and new, who reject the Old Testament as the book of the Jews and not of the Christians believe in a different Christ and preach a different gospel. They were excommunicated in the ancient church. Modern Protestant theologians such as Friedrich Schleiermacher and Adolf von Harnack represented a similar disparagement of the Old Testament as outdated and no longer valid for modern Christians. The same view was taken over by the German Christians who supported the anti-Jewish policies of the National Socialists under Hitler.

The Bible is valued for many reasons; it is used as a book of devotions, as a source of doctrines, or as a record of history. But what makes the Bible unique and authoritative for Christianity is the fact that Christ is its central content, "the way, the truth, and the life" (John 14:16). The idea of Christ as the criterion of biblical faith has been supported by theologians of many different schools of thought. For Karl Barth, God's self-revelation is knowable only through Christ; for Oscar Cullmann, Christ is the midpoint of the biblical history of salvation *(Heilsgeschichte)*; for Rudolf

---

19. *Luther's Works,* vol. 35, ed. E. Theodore Bachman (Philadelphia: Fortress Press, 1960), p. 236.

Bultmann, the Christ-event is the exclusive content of the apostolic *kerygma;* for Paul Tillich, the affirmation that Jesus is the Christ, the bringer of the new being, makes Christianity what it is; for Wolfhart Pannenberg, the resurrection of Jesus is the proleptic event of the eschatological end of history. On account of Christ *(propter Christum)* the church regards the Bible as the norm of its sacred teachings and as the reason for its practice of preaching from biblical pericopes. The christological content of the Bible puts it in a class of its own. No other great book of religion, literature, or philosophy can match the Bible in the perspective of the church, chiefly on account of its instrumental function in authoring faith in the living Christ of apostolic preaching.

Without the reference point of faith it is meaningless to call the Bible the Word of God. This does not mean that every single thing in the Bible is the Word of God as an isolated datum or that some things, say, the red-letter passages introduced by "God said" or "Jesus said," are the Word of God. It is more appropriate to hold that the whole Bible is the Word of God because it frames the story of God's dealings with Israel and the church, the main point of which is Jesus Christ. No church theologian has said it more clearly than Martin Luther:

> All the genuine sacred books agree in this, that all of them preach and inculcate *(treiben)* Christ. And that is the true test by which to judge all books, when we see whether or not they inculcate Christ. For all the Scriptures show us Christ (Romans 3:21); and St. Paul will know nothing but Christ (I Cor. 2:2). Whatever does not teach Christ is not yet apostolic, even though St. Peter or St. Paul does the teaching. Again, whatever preaches Christ would be apostolic, even if Judas, Annas, Pilate, and Herod were doing it.[20]

Here we have Luther's famous formula, *"was Christum treibt"* — what inculcates or drives Christ home.

A Christ-centered hermeneutic that accepts Luther's idea that the books of the Old Testament are the cradle of Christ is the best antidote against the bibliolatry of Protestant fundamentalism, which tends to

---

20. "Prefaces to the New Testament," *Luther's Works,* vol. 35, p. 396.

worship the cradle. The Reformers had such a high regard for the Bible because of its message of salvation through the life, death, and resurrection of Jesus Christ. The church's theology has not been helped much by attributing superlative adjectives to the Bible, speaking of it as infallible and inerrant. The Scriptures are perfectly clear with respect to their purpose of conveying the revelation of the living God for the salvation of the world.

## The Problem of Historical Revelation

The idea of God revealing himself through the Bible has been a problem for theology ever since the rise of historical criticism in the eighteenth century. The reason for this is that, according to the Bible, God's revelation is linked to historical events. Jesus of Nazareth is a person who lived at a particular time and place. John 1:14 says that "the Word became flesh and lived among us." The Word of God appeared as a person in history. Only if the revelation of God were like a universal truth of reason or law of nature could it be dissociated from the historical situation in which it arose. If the biblical writings were not interpretations of historical facts, there would be no problem of historical revelation. The fight between the negative and positive biblical critics would be pointless, because faith would be unconcerned about the historicity of the events that mediate the revelation of God.

But faith in the God of the Bible is essentially linked to the historical medium through which God reveals himself. The object of inquiry for modern historical criticism is the medium, not the revelation of God as such. Historical research as such is a-theistic with respect to the idea of God revealing himself. What happens to faith when critical historiography writes the historical media of biblical revelation out of existence? What if it concludes that the New Testament picture of Jesus as the Christ is mostly a distortion, as the "Jesus Seminar" claims? Would this spell the ultimate defeat of the faith confessed by historic Christianity? This is precisely the professed motivation of the leaders of the "Jesus Seminar" — Robert Funk, John Dominic Crossan, and Marcus Borg. Funk writes, "It is a good thing that the true historical Jesus should overthrow the Christ of Christian orthodoxy, the Christ of the creeds. . . . Finally, it has become clear that even the Christ of the Gospels is a further impediment to any serious effort to rediscover Jesus of Nazareth."[21] Any theology that aims to be Christian cannot remain indifferent to the historicity of its basis and content. Funk believes that the "Jesus Seminar" has pulled the historical rug out from under the interpretations of faith given by the Gospels and transmitted by the creeds of the church.

The Christian faith is oriented to Jesus of Nazareth as the evangelists and apostles pictured him in the New Testament Gospels and Epistles. It is a mistake to think that the results of historical research, whether conducted by conservative or liberal scholars, can verify or falsify the basic Christian confession that Jesus of Nazareth is the Christ of God. Faith is not based on a sum of hypothetical facts established by historical inquiry into "what really happened" behind the Gospels. Authentic Christian faith is radically dependent on the apostolic witness to Jesus as the Christ and not on the learned opinion of biblical scholars, no matter who they are. Faith does not base itself on scientific reconstructions of the *nuda facta* underlying the apostolic kerygmatic testimonies. However, faith is based on Jesus so far as his personal identity and meaning are proclaimed in the witnesses of the first believers and transmitted to all succeeding generations with self-authenticating spiritual power. Making the decision of faith when confronted by the biblical picture of Jesus as the Christ is no easier or harder for the learned theologian than for the simplest Christian. A professor's historical erudition does not bring him or her to faith, and lack of knowledge in the servant who sweeps the floor is not an impediment to faith in Jesus as Savior. That Jesus is the Christ of God is a proposition a person either accepts or rejects as a judgment of faith and not as the end-product of historical investigation.

The referral of faith to the New Testament apostolic *kerygma* includes what it conveys about Jesus as an essential element of it. The *kerygma* without Jesus is void, and Jesus without the *kerygma* is meaningless. That is to say, the real Jesus is the content of the *kerygma*. The essential features of the earthly Jesus have been inextricably incorporated into the apostolic memory of his mission and significance. Putative his-

---

21. Robert Funk, *Honest to Jesus* (San Francisco: HarperSanFrancisco, 1996), p. 20.

torical facts concerning Jesus that are not part of the New Testament record of apostolic preaching are irrelevant to Christian faith, because they have had nothing to do with the founding of the church and its life in the Spirit. The church has exemplified a true instinct in its history by always preaching from the Bible and not from the gnostic Gospels, or the Muslim (Qur'an), Hindu (Upanishads), or Buddhist (Bhagavad-Gita) Scriptures. Every pericope selected for preaching focuses on some aspect of the total biblical picture of Jesus as the Christ of God.

New Testament scholarship rightly points out the diversity of theologies in the New Testament. Paul's theology is different from John's, and each of the Synoptic Gospels differs from the others. Still they are united in their unanimous witness to Jesus as the Christ and as Lord and Savior. This is what counts for faith, despite the fact that scholars disagree on what Jesus thought about himself. Did Jesus understand himself as the Son of Man, as the Messiah, as the Son of God, or as the Savior who came to die for the sins of the world? It is salutary to know that faith is dependent on the primitive apostolic witnesses, not on the current consensus among scholars. A picture of Jesus deprived of his messianic self-consciousness is not the picture of Jesus as the Christ portrayed in the Gospels and the entire New Testament. Some scholars think they have uncovered a non-messianic Jesus behind the Gospels. Theirs is the "so-called historical Jesus" that Kähler rejected.

The access we have to the real Jesus of history is solely through the picture of faith left behind by the apostles, a picture that includes the double ending of his life, first the cross and then the resurrection. The historical-critical attempt to discover the empirical truth about the life of Jesus ends with his crucifixion and relegates the story of the resurrection to myth or legend. It functions with too narrow a concept of history. This leads us to the question of the next chapter: Did Jesus of Nazareth really rise from the dead?

## Questions for Discussion

1. How would you characterize the chief difference between faith and reason when it comes to knowing God or Christ?

2. Luther said, "I believe that by my own reason or strength I cannot believe in Jesus Christ, my Lord, or come to him. But the Holy Spirit has called me through the Gospel." Who is this Holy Spirit? And how does the Holy Spirit work?

3. What is your view of historians who believe they can know who Jesus really is apart from faith and the testimony of the Holy Spirit?

4. What do you think is the proper role of the historical-critical method in the interpretation of the Bible? What can it accomplish?

5. What does it mean to confess that the Bible is the Word of God? What are the implications in saying that the Bible is the book of the church?

6. Hermeneutics is the art of interpretation. What are the essential links in the "hermeneutical chain" applicable in the interpretation of the Bible?

7. Søren Kierkegaard asked, "How do we become contemporary with Christ?" What do you think he meant by the question? How would you answer the question as you understand it?

# III

# Did Jesus Really Rise from the Dead?

A t the center of the Christian message is the good news that God raised Jesus of Nazareth from the dead. This is what the New Testament calls the "gospel," the announcement of God's act to deliver humanity from the finality of death (1 Cor. 15:26). For the first Christians — the disciples and apostles of Jesus — there was no gospel worth preaching or believing without the resurrection of Jesus. There would have been no Christianity, no church, and no Christians if the resurrection of Jesus had not happened. This is a historical fact that every reasonable historian will acknowledge. A historian who is not a believer cannot help but observe the fact that belief in Jesus as the risen Lord permeated every aspect of the early church's life and thought.

So what is the problem? The application of the modern historical-critical method in the study of the Bible, beginning with the Enlightenment, released a flood of doubts regarding the stories of Jesus' resurrection in the Gospels. Hermann Samuel Reimarus (1694-1768), an eighteenth-century German professor of Hebrew and Oriental languages, cast doubt on the Easter stories by observing their many discrepancies. So he concluded that they are little more than pure fiction.[1] David Friedrich Strauss (1808-1874) followed suit, scandalizing the Christian world by calling into question the historicity of the Easter event. He did not doubt that the early Christians believed the Easter stories as factual reports. But as primitive

---

1. See Charles H. Talbert, ed., *Reimarus: Fragments* (Philadelphia: Fortress Press, 1970).

people they were deluded; they were susceptible to belief in miracles. But enlightened scholars working with the assumptions of historical science are convinced that nothing happens beyond natural causation. If they believe in God at all, they are deists who believe that God does not and cannot perform acts within the order of creation. Once God created the world, he let it run according to its own built-in natural laws. Hence, scientific historiography must explain the early Christian belief in Jesus' resurrection without appealing to a miraculous intervention of God.[2] Rather quickly the wider reading public became exposed to the notion that the Easter stories were fabricated out of legends and myths.

Many still clung to the idea that it is possible to be Christian without believing in the resurrection of Jesus. Christians can still be inspired by the words and acts of Jesus and his heroic death on the cross. In this view, the name of Jesus refers to a person dead and gone, remembered by some for his unforgettable personality and moral teachings. As such he is not the living Christ presently active in the world through his church and the members of the body of which he is head. For most of Christian history the words of the apostle Paul have been decisive: "If Christ has not been raised, then our proclamation has been in vain and your faith has been in vain. . . . If Christ has not been raised, your faith is futile and you are still in your sins. . . . If for this life only we have hoped in Christ, we are of all people most to be pitied" (1 Cor. 15:14, 17, 19).

But since the Enlightenment some theologians are attempting to reinvent Christianity without the resurrection. A few examples will suffice. A. J. M. Wedderburn, New Testament professor at the University of Munich, wrote: "Paul's logic simply cannot hold water today. His rhetoric has led him astray."[3] The title of his book is *Beyond Resurrection*, and its thesis is that the results of historical criticism have made it impossible for us moderns to believe that God raised Jesus from the dead. David Griffin, a systematician from the school of process theology, wrote: "Christian faith (as I understand it) is possible apart from belief in Jesus'

---

2. David Friedrich Strauss, *The Life of Jesus Critically Examined,* ed. Peter Hodgson (Philadelphia: Westminster Press, 1972).

3. A. J. M. Wedderburn, *Beyond Resurrection* (Peabody: Hendrickson, 1999), p. 154.

resurrection in particular and life beyond bodily death in general, and because of the widespread skepticism regarding these traditional beliefs, they should be presented as optional."[4] Robert Funk, speaking for the "Jesus Seminar," wrote: "The Fellows reached a fairly firm consensus: Belief in Jesus' resurrection did not depend on what happened to his corpse. They are supported in this by the judgment of many contemporary scholars. Jesus' resurrection did not involve the resuscitation of a dead body. About three-fourths of the Fellows believe that Jesus' followers did not know what happened to his body."[5] In answer to the question of what the resurrection meant to the first Christians, Funk offers this answer: "To claim that Jesus rose from the dead is a way of confessing that Jesus revealed what the world was really like, that he caught a glimpse of eternity. Affirmation of Jesus' resurrection should send his devotees searching through his parables and aphorisms for traces of that glimpse."[6] For Funk the Christian faith was founded on a glimpse. This would be hilarious if it were not so much empty talk.

## The Resurrection as History

Traditionally Christians have believed and understood the resurrection to be an historical event, something that happened in space and time, not in some heavenly realm out of sight. The Easter stories agree that Jesus appeared and was seen by eyewitnesses after his death and burial. However, they also suggest that the person they saw after Easter was different from the One they knew before Easter. Some kind of transformation had occurred, so much so that the category of "history" can hardly do it justice. By his resurrection Jesus experienced a glorification of his body, taking on a new mode of existence. Hence, it is appropriate to say that while the resurrection is a historical event, it is also more than that. It is at the same time an eschatological event, meaning that Jesus was on his way from time to eternity, never to return to his pre-resurrection

---

4. David Griffin, *Process Christology* (Philadelphia: Westminster Press, 1973), p. 12.

5. Robert W. Funk, *Honest to Jesus* (New York: Harper Collins, 1996), p. 259.

6. Funk, *Honest to Jesus,* p. 313.

form of physical existence. I believe this is a reasonable conclusion to draw from a careful reading of the Easter texts.

Given that the resurrection of Jesus is both a historical and an eschatological event, both reason and faith work together to affirm its truth and meaning. The application of the historical-critical method by itself cannot prove that God raised Jesus from the dead. Neither is the confession of Jesus' resurrection accomplished simply by a blind leap of faith. I agree with a statement made by Alan Richardson: "Apart from faith in the divine revelation through the biblical history, such as will enable us to declare with conviction that Christ is risen indeed, the judgment that the resurrection of Jesus is an historical event is unlikely to be made, since the rational motive for making it will be absent."[7] Critical historians of Christian origins will not likely conclude from the evidence, after examining the stories of the empty tomb and of Jesus' post-Easter appearances, that the resurrection really happened, unless they at the same time believe it and participate in the church's celebration of the Lord's presence through Word and Sacrament. Faith opens the eyes of reason to grasp the truth of the good news that God raised Jesus from the dead.

## Resurrection as Eschatology

To summarize what we have said so far, Easter faith is the conviction that Jesus is no longer dead but alive. The resurrection is a historical event insofar as it happened in a definite place, in a tomb somewhere in Jerusalem, and at a definite time, a few short days after Jesus' death. But the resurrection is also an eschatological event. It signals a new beginning that put an end to a life that advanced toward death and inaugurated a new order of life that dies no more. This is the start of an answer to the "so what?" question. So what if Jesus lived again after he died: what difference does that make for all of us who still have to face our deaths? If we fail to answer this question clearly, the resurrection will cease to re-

---

7. Alan Richardson, *History Sacred and Profane* (Philadelphia: Westminster Press, 1964), p. 212.

main central in Christian theology and preaching. This in fact happened in the second century. The resurrection became no longer integral in the experiential piety of Christians. The Hebraic idea of resurrection was replaced by the Hellenistic notion of immortality. In many subsequent Christologies the theme of the resurrection lagged far behind its position in New Testament Christianity. Generally in Western theology the cross eclipsed the resurrection; the main stress was on the atoning death of Jesus on Calvary. Salvation was envisioned chiefly in terms of reconciliation from guilt and atonement for sin, effected by the vicarious sufferings and death of Jesus. The death of Jesus as a sacrifice or satisfaction accomplished salvation without any essential connection with the resurrection.[8] Anglican theology placed a heavy emphasis on the incarnation; liberal Protestant theology directed its soteriological focus away from the cross and resurrection of Jesus to his earthly life and moral teachings.

Recent developments in biblical exegesis and systematic theology have seen a resurgence of resurrection language. Historical criticism of the New Testament has established beyond reasonable doubt that faith in the risen Jesus is the point of departure and main focus of primitive Christianity. Without the Easter faith there would have been no gospel and no church. The belief that God raised Jesus from the dead on the third day is as old as the Christian faith. The most skeptical historians will agree with this, even if the resurrection is not a belief they share. To rethink the Christian faith in light of the consensus that the primitive Christian message was founded on the Easter faith and that the entire story of Jesus in the Gospels was told from its perspective, it is necessary to demonstrate its existential meaning for people today. It is necessary but not sufficient to assert that the resurrection of Jesus is an event of history. As an eschatological event the resurrection correlates with the universal human hope — expressed in various ways in virtually all religions — for life beyond the finality of death.

The expression "resurrection from the dead" is a metaphor. Just as people arise from sleep in the morning, so shall the dead arise from their graves. Eschatological hope for a resurrection from the dead emerged in

---

8. This point is clearly demonstrated by Gustaf Aulén in his little classic *Christus Victor*, tr. A. G. Hebert (New York: Macmillan, 1951).

the apocalyptic writings of post-exilic Judaism. The Jewish contemporaries of Jesus shared the apocalyptic expectation of resurrection. The question is: Do we? Is any such hope still meaningful for us today? Many modern people seem to have no problem believing in some kind of immortality, reincarnation, transmigration, or metempsychosis, some kind of passage of the soul from this life to another, into another person or perhaps even an animal. Christians who take their bearings from the Bible do not believe that. They do not believe a person is a soul without a body. Christians believe in the resurrection of the body, not the immortality of the soul. They base their belief on Jesus' resurrection as a "spiritual body," not a perishable physical body, but a new immortal spiritual body. Paul's term was *sōma pneumatikos*.[9]

Paul's view is just as existentially relevant today as it was for the first Christians. Resurrection hope holds that this earthly mortal body will be transformed into a new mode of existence. The transformation is radical; all is new, yet there is an essential personal continuity between the present physical body and the new form of life in a risen body. People by nature hope for fulfillment of their personal identity beyond death, restlessly seeking a final destiny beyond the limits of finitude. Augustine (354-430) said it best in his prayer: "For thou hast made us for thyself and restless is our heart until it comes to rest in thee."[10]

Hope for life beyond death is not exclusive to Christians. No doubt, just as there will always be some who deny the existence of God, so there will likely always be some who manage to quash hope for eternal life, who exist as nihilists without hope. As creatures of time and history, human beings live toward the future. They cannot live in the past or put a stop to time. But if there is no future beyond death to anticipate, humans are doomed to move forward into the jaws of death. Our wager is that hope for fulfillment beyond death is a structural dimension of human existence and that precisely this attribute formulates the necessary condition of contemporary belief in the gospel of Jesus' resurrection from the dead.

9. 1 Cor. 15:42-44: "So is it with the resurrection of the dead. What is sown is perishable, what is raised is imperishable. It is sown in dishonor, it is raised in glory. It is sown in weakness, it is raised in power. It is sown a physical body, it is raised a spiritual body."

10. Augustine, *Confessions,* tr. and ed. Albert C. Outler (online version), I.1.1.

## Implications of Resurrection Hope

Many people face death without hope. Secularism is the philosophy that says this world is all there is. What you see is what you get, nothing more. Yet the most secular of modern people seem to be just as afraid to die as ancient and primitive people. They suppress the question of death or drown it out with drugs, noise, sex, busyness, or anything else to desensitize their fear of the unknowable future mingled with dread, despair, and anxiety. Existentialist philosophers have filled their writings analyzing such moods. Meanwhile, naturalistic philosophers assure us that there is absolutely nothing to fear in death. Death is merely the necessary end for every creature living within the eco-system of nature, no different for humans than for plants and animals.

Naturalists who spend their time in science laboratories cannot help but observe that every living thing shares in the physiological process of decay and disintegration. From this perspective death is perfectly natural. It should pose neither terror nor mystery. But it does. No amount of assurance that death is natural can dispel the distress that accompanies it when a loved one dies. There is something supra-natural and theological about death and dying, expressed biblically in the statement, "The wages of sin is death" (Rom. 6:23). Of course, naturalists would claim there is no such thing as sin. That is because "sin" is itself a theological concept; it defines the human condition under the wrath and judgment of God. Where there is no God, there is no sin. Sin is existing in a wrong relationship to God. The reality of sin transforms the sense of one's natural mortality into a transcendent fear of the deadly, destructive, and damnable power of death. It is as though one could see through the veil of death to the other side and see the face of a wrathful God. Jonathan Edwards (1703-1758) preached his most famous sermon entitled, "Sinners in the Hands of an Angry God."[11] Of course, that kind of preaching has fallen out of fashion. Now preaching is more like what H. Richard Niebuhr (1894-1962) observed in liberal Protestantism: "A God without

---

11. The sermon is available in tract form from International Outreach, Inc., P.O. Box 1286, Ames, Iowa, 50014, and online through the Jonathan Edwards Center of Yale University (http://edwards.yale.edu/).

wrath brought men without sin into a kingdom without judgment through the ministrations of a Christ without a cross."[12]

The good news of the resurrection is that it liberates us from bondage to the fear of death. We still have to die, but resurrection hope robs death of its enslaving fear. Because God raised Jesus from the dead, we have reason to hope and trust that the promise of life is more powerful in the end than death. We are free to hope for a lasting future of life with God and with all those whom the love of God embraces. The hope of the resurrection concerns each individual person. Eschatological hope is about total personal fulfillment, making a difference in how Christians live here and now. The power of the resurrection in personal life overcomes the feeling that a person's life is lived for naught. It gives a sense of a meaningful outcome of our lives, of the worthwhileness of our efforts in spite of our sins and failures. We cannot derive this from anything in the world around us. Nothing in this world can mediate the love, healing, freedom, and righteousness that humans long for in the midst of their brokenness. On account of the resurrection of Jesus, the value of each individual life — including each little one of history, especially the little one yet unborn — becomes boundless and infinite.

The scope of resurrection hope is as wide as the world. It is a total hope, embracing the future of society and the world. There is a wideness in God's mercy that generates a universalism of hope. At the end God will be all in all,[13] totally present in everyone and everything that Christ has redeemed. This is no puny hope that clings merely to the salvation of the individual soul. Paul's vision of hope embraces communal and cosmic dimensions beyond all human imagination. This means that Christians imbued with the love of God hope not merely for themselves, their families, and their friends, but for the whole family of humankind and the whole of creation. We can speak of such things only in the language of symbols. Not only the history of humanity, but also the history of nature is heir to the biblical promise of fulfillment. The gospel is not good news for humans and bad news for the world. Humans live in continuity with

---

12. H. Richard Niebuhr, *The Kingdom of God in America* (New York: Harper and Brothers, 1937), p. 150.

13. 1 Cor. 15:28.

first Christians were all Jews. For them to call Jesus the Messiah meant that he was God's mediator of salvation, not that he was the Son of God, let alone sharing the same essence as God the Father. It took the ancient church a long time, and only after numerous stormy controversies, to confess the full divinity of Jesus.

New Testament scholars are still debating whether Jesus revealed himself as the Messiah to any of his friends and followers. We will leave that question aside because it is one that scarcely makes a particle of difference to the Christian faith. What is clear is that Jesus did not wish to be understood as the kind of Messiah many Jews were expecting at that time, a warrior who would deliver Israel from Roman oppression by means of armed insurrection. Jesus was not a Zealot, a member of a radical patriotic group that advocated the overthrow of Roman rule. Jesus directed his fiercest criticisms against some of his own people, especially the Sadducees and Pharisees, rather than against the Roman occupation. According to Mark's Gospel, Jesus admitted that he was the Messiah only when he was led as a prisoner before the High Priest. But Jesus was not the political Messiah that the Jews were hoping for. The Jews did not expect their Messiah to have to suffer and be killed. A crucified Messiah was a contradiction in terms — a scandal to the Jews. But for the apostle Paul that is the essence of the good news.

A second title is "Lord," in Greek *kyrios*. It has two uses, as a polite form of address like "Dear Sir" when addressing a letter, and as a name that refers to God in the Old Testament. When the Old Testament was translated from Hebrew into Greek, *kyrios* was used to translate the holy name of God. Joel 2:32 states: "Whoever calls upon the name of the Lord will be saved." The Lord is God. In the New Testament Acts 2:36 states that "everyone who calls on the name of the Lord will be saved," and here "the Lord" refers to Jesus. This is an example of an early process of development whereby names and attributes that refer to God in the Old Testament are transferred to Jesus in the New Testament. God is Lord; Jesus is Lord. God saves; Jesus saves. In the mind of the early church the actions of God and of Jesus are spoken of in the same breath. Titles of exaltation that properly belong to God Almighty are used to describe the elevated status of Jesus in the post-Easter situation. It was on account of the combined impact of the resurrection of Jesus and the outpouring of the

the natural environment. Ultimately the forward movement of the material world and the history of personal and social life converge on the eschatological future of God, a future that is proleptically present in Jesus. These are but a few of the intimations of glory that God has in store for humanity and the world on account of raising Jesus from the dead.

## Questions for Discussion

1. The word "resurrection" is a metaphor commonly used in various contexts — sports, politics, etc. What is your image of an occurrence referred to by the word "resurrection"?

2. Some theologians assert that belief in the resurrection of Jesus should be considered optional for Christians today because, they say, miracles are incredible in light of modern science. What is your understanding of a miracle? What makes belief in miracles difficult for modern people?

3. Christian traditions emphasize different aspects of the life of Jesus Christ. Some place great stress on the crucifixion, others on the incarnation or the ascension, still others on Jesus' moral teachings. The Eastern Orthodox are noted for their emphasis on the good news of Easter, the resurrection of Jesus. Where do you tend to place the emphasis in your picture of Jesus?

4. If we should say that the resurrection of Jesus is a historical event, are we using the word "historical" in a straightforward, matter-of-fact sense? Explain.

5. How radical would the transformation of traditional Christianity be if belief in the resurrection were eliminated?

6. What does it mean to say that the resurrection of Jesus is an eschatological event?

7. How does the resurrection of Jesus give meaning and content to the Christian hope for the future?

# IV

## *Why Do Christians Believe That Jesus Is "Truly God"?*

Jesus of Nazareth was a man, a human being, a Palestinian Jew of the first century. All the ancient Christian creeds affirm the true humanity of Jesus. The Apostles' Creed confesses that Jesus "was crucified, died, and was buried." The Nicene Creed confesses that Jesus Christ "became incarnate from the virgin Mary, and was made man." The Creed of Chalcedon (A.D. 451) adds more words, saying that Jesus Christ is "perfect in manhood . . . truly man . . . with a rational soul and a body . . . and of the same reality as we are ourselves as far as his humanness is concerned, thus like us in all respects, sin only excepted."

Why did these early creeds insist so strongly on the full humanity of Jesus, something that seems beyond doubt today? The Gospels tell the story of Jesus of Nazareth as a human being, but by the end of the first century he was remembered as something more than a mere mortal. How much more? For most of five centuries the ancient church wrestled with the question of the true identity of Jesus of Nazareth. It reached the conclusion that Jesus was by nature fully human and was also personally divine. But for centuries theologians struggled over how best to think Jesus as a person with two contrasting natures, human and divine. It important to remember that at the start the first Christians did not speak about Jesus in the way the later creeds did, as "God from God true God from true God . . . of one Being with the Father," using many similar phrases. The most common title for Jesus that the first generation of believers used was "Messiah," or "Christ," its Greek equivalent.

Holy Spirit at Pentecost that the early church confessed the divinity of Jesus Christ. We can observe a trajectory of sanctified imagination that starts with the memory of Jesus the Man of Nazareth, a teacher, preacher, and healer; and then, impacted by the double ending of Jesus' life in the cross and resurrection, it moves to confession of Jesus as the crucified Messiah; and at last it reaches the doxological language of worship that glorifies and praises Jesus as really and truly God.

Another title that the New Testament uses to refer to Jesus is "Son of God." The Old Testament speaks of "sons of God" in the plural to refer to all people. The New Testament refers to Jesus as "Son of God" in an exclusive sense. He is *the* Son of God, signifying something unique about his relation to God. Believers are also "sons of God," but only by adoption. Jesus' extremely close relationship to God was implied when he addressed God intimately as *Abba*. This special Father-Son relationship was later to play a huge role in the construction of the doctrine of the Trinity. We believe in God the Father and in Jesus Christ his only Son our Lord. Here we have in a single sentence the three most important titles of exaltation bestowed on Jesus: Christ, Son, and Lord.

## The Logic of Salvation

The "logic of salvation"[1] is at work behind the scenes in bringing about the equation of Jesus with the being of God. We believe the Holy Spirit was at work in the early church to illumine the minds of Jesus' followers to acknowledge who he *was* on the basis of what he *did*. For Philip Melanchthon (1497-1560), Luther's fellow reformer, this idea was a principle of theological method, which he expressed by his most famous utterance: "To know Christ is to know his benefits." Who Jesus is refers to his identity, his personal being. The word "ontology" denotes this aspect of Christology. The fourth-century Creed of Nicaea uses ontological language in speaking of Jesus: "We believe in One Lord, Jesus Christ, the only Son of God, eternally begotten of the Father, God from God, Light from

---

1. "Soteriology" is the technical theological word for what we are calling the "logic of salvation."

Light, true God from true God, begotten not made, of one Being with the Father." That is an ontological recitation of the identity of Jesus as God. Another example of ontological Christology that places Jesus on a par with God is in the fifth-century Creed of Chalcedon: "We all with one voice teach that it should be confessed that our Lord Jesus Christ is one and the same Son, the same perfect in Godhead, the same perfect in manhood, truly God and truly man, the same consisting of a rational soul and a body; of one substance *(homoousios)* with the Father as to his Godhead and the same of one substance *(homoousios)* with us as to his manhood." *Homoousios* is the Greek word used to identify Jesus fully as God and equally fully as human.

Some have criticized the Nicene Creed for using a non-biblical term that comes from Greek philosophy to speak about Jesus. The Council Fathers, led by Athanasius, chose *homoousios* to combat another term — *homoiousios* — that was being used by Arius and his supporters to speak of Jesus' identity. The difference between the two words is merely an iota, but a crucial one: *homoousios* means "of the same substance" and *homoiousios* means "of similar substance." One historian observed that laypeople would gather in coffeehouses and argue over an iota. For the church fathers the entire burden of salvation rests on the huge difference an iota makes. In his book *The Decline and Fall of the Roman Empire,* Edward Gibbon (1737-1794) stated that never before had so much fuss been made over a single letter of the alphabet. The question has lost none of its critical importance for contemporary Christians: Is Jesus God or is he god-like? Is he the God-man, the subject of a real incarnation of God, or is he a godly person, the last in a long line of Hebrew prophets or one of the saints?

The early Christians did not start their thinking with the high dogmatic Christology of Nicaea and Chalcedon. They started their christological thinking from their experience of what Jesus meant to them, of what he accomplished for them and their salvation. They started with soteriology, what we call the "logic of salvation." The Jews in Jesus' time were monotheists: they believed that God is one. Further, the people of Israel believed that only God can save. Whether as slaves in Egypt or captives in Babylon, they knew they could not liberate themselves. The Jews in Jesus' day, of course, held the same belief: only God can save. But soon after Easter we read of a small band of Jews confessing that Jesus saves. "And there is salvation in no one else, for there is no other name under heaven given among men by which we must be saved" (Acts 4:12). Jesus will save his people from their sins, something only God can do.

Similarly, as monotheists the Jews learned from their ancient prophets that idolatry was the greatest of sins. No one other than God is to be worshipped. Jews were clear that no creature should be worshipped. That would be idolatry. Worship of a mere human being would be anthropolatry. The early Christians refused to worship Caesar, the Roman emperor, and were thrown to the lions. Hence, it must have been quite a shocking reversal when Jewish believers in Jesus "called on the name of the Lord Jesus Christ" (1 Cor. 1:2). Jews who became Christians not only continued to worship God, but worshipped Jesus as God. Jesus is depicted as exercising the functions that typically for the Hebrews belong only to God. God saves; Jesus saves. God forgives; Jesus forgives. God is at the center of worship; Jesus is also placed at the center of worship. Jesus reveals God. Jesus represents God, so much so that he becomes the sum and substance of the gospel the church proclaims to the nations.

As Christians and churches we do not have anything else of unique and universal significance to offer the world. We do not offer a better political ideology, a more successful economic system, or a more sophisticated philosophy. We do not have better solutions to the problems of over-population, environmental pollution, world hunger, global warming, illegal immigration, and so forth. We have been given a gospel to tell to the nations. If we water that down, people will soon suspect that we stand for nothing of universal and eternal importance. Already in Jesus' lifetime people were buzzing about who he is: "By what authority are you doing these things, and who gave you this authority?" (Matt. 21:23). "Who is this, who even forgives sins?" (Luke 7:49). "Who then is this, that even wind and sea obey him?" (Mark 4:41). Remembering this remarkable person and his deeds, the early Christians drew the Spirit-inspired conclusion that Jesus must have been all along Immanuel, God with us, the Son of God incarnate. By the fourth century a church assembly at Nicaea (A.D. 325) asserted of Jesus that he shares the nature of God the Father, "God of God, Light of Light, Very God of Very God." A subsequent assembly in Constantinople (381) added that Jesus was "born of the Father before all time." These are astounding assertions. Liberal Protestant theologians from Schleiermacher to Ritschl and from Harnack to Bultmann have declared that, given the modern scientific picture of the world, it is impossible for people today to believe that a Palestinian Jew who lived some two thousand years ago and suffered a criminal's death on a cross could have preexisted in God's eternity as the foundation and beginning of all things. Yet, despite what some theologians may think, the church has retained these beliefs in its creeds and liturgies, in fidelity to the Scriptures and ancient Christian tradition. Capitulation to the naturalistic worldview of modern science would put an end not only to the symbols and concepts of the church's high Christology; it would equally prohibit all theological thought and language, including the very idea of God. Atheism would be the logical outcome of such a reductionistic operation.

## Low and High Christology

Orthodox Christianity continues to affirm a "high Christology" that teaches that Jesus was not only a good man but also the God-man, not only godly or god-like but "very God of very God." For a "high Christology" the difference between Jesus and the rest of us is one of *kind.* The difference is absolute. For a "low Christology" the difference between Jesus and the rest of us is one of *degree.* The difference is merely relative. He is simply a better person, more religious, more holy, and more moral. If that were all, we would have no sufficient reason to call him the "Savior of humankind." For only God can save humans from the transcendental tyrants of sin, death, and the devil.

Three versions of "low Christology" were created and circulated within various communities in the ancient church. Needless to say, they have their advocates among theologians today. One version is called Ebionism, a second-century movement that regarded Jesus as a mere man, denying his divinity altogether. We know of the Ebionites not from their writings, of which we have none, but only through the polemical writings of their orthodox critics. Most of the ancient christological heresies were named after a heretic, like Arius, Nestorius, Eutyches, Apollinaris, Sabellius, and so forth. But Ebionism was not named after a heretic called Ebion. No such person existed. The word comes from the Hebrew *ebionim*, meaning "poor." The Ebionites came mainly from a poorer class of Jews. They believed that Jesus was certainly the Messiah, but he was only a man, not the Son of God. They also denied the virgin birth of Jesus. Jesus was born the natural child of an earthly father and mother, they said, Joseph and Mary.

The second version of a "low Christology" is adoptionism. Adoptionist Christology is what the term suggests: Jesus became the Son of God by adoption. He was not so from the beginning, not the only begotten Son of God from all eternity. By the indwelling of the Holy Spirit he became the beloved Son of his Father by gradual spiritual and moral growth in holiness. This kind of adoptionist Christology was taught by Paul of Samosata, bishop of Antioch. In those days just as today, it seems, bishops enjoyed no immunity from heresy.

The third version of a "low Christology" was Arianism, named after Arius (ca. 256-336), a presbyter in Alexandria. Arius was neither an Ebionite nor an adoptionist. His Christology was notably higher. For Arius Jesus was more than a human being and more than an adopted Son of God. In fact Arius sounded so biblical and Christ-centered that for a long time the majority of bishops and theologians supported his teaching, even including the Arian pope, Honorius I, who was condemned as a heretic by the sixth general council in 680. But Arius met a fiercely orthodox opponent in Athanasius (293-373), bishop of Alexandria. The controversy between Arius and Athanasius was classic in its significance for all subsequent churchly theology. For Arius Jesus was the Son of God who existed with the Father before the creation of the world, but not God. Jesus did not share the divine essence; he was not eternal. Arius's favorite theological phrase, one that Arians chanted in a hymn, was: "There was when he was not." In the beginning there was God alone; that was to preserve monotheism. Then God created the Logos, the "Word" referred to in the prologue of the Gospel of John: "In the beginning was the Word, and the Word was with God, and the Word was God. He was in the beginning with God; all things were made through him, and without him was not anything made that was made" (John 1:1-3). Arius had no problem quoting those verses, except for the clause "and the Word was God." For Arius the Word was created by God to assist in creating the world. The Word, Arius said, was the "firstborn of all creation," and therefore a creature. When John 1:14 says that "the Word became flesh," according to Arius only a created being appeared in the flesh. Hence, there was no real incarnation of God. Athanasius countered, saying that, if there was no real incarnation of the Word, if the Word that became flesh was not truly and really God, there could be no real salvation. If Jesus is not God, forget about calling him the Savior. For only God, and no creature, has the power to save.

It is clearly taught throughout the New Testament writings and in the classical creeds of the church that Jesus is not *a* Savior, one among many, but the one and only Savior of the world. He is absolutely unique in terms of who he is and what he does. The hope of salvation for humanity and the world rests on him, for "at the name of Jesus every knee should bow, in heaven and on earth and under the earth, and every tongue confess that Jesus Christ is Lord, to the glory of God the Father" (Phil. 2:10). Take this away or water it down, and the whole Jesus-movement that went forward from Jerusalem, into Judea and Samaria, and eventually to the ends of the earth, will simply peter out. People will quit going to church and the churches will lose members. This is exactly what is happening all over Europe and in the United States at the present time. It may be only a coincidence but at least it should be a warning that bad theology can have disastrous consequences.

Is it possible to have too high a Christology? Yes, if one were to emphasize the divinity of Christ at the expense of his humanity. There was a heresy in the ancient church called "docetism." It was the very opposite of Ebionism. Its name comes from the Greek word *dokein,* meaning "to seem." Docetism taught that Jesus only *seemed* to be a real human being. Jesus looked human, but only because he appeared wearing a human mask. He was really a divine figure masquerading as a man. Not so, said the fathers and doctors of the church. To be sure, Jesus was truly God, but he was also truly human, "of the same substance with us as to his human nature, in all things like unto us, except without sin" (the Creed of Chalcedon). Jesus grew up like other Jewish boys in Palestine. We have very little biographical information on the first thirty years of Jesus' life.

We are told merely that as a man he got thirsty and hungry like everyone else. He got tired and needed to rest like everyone else. He suffered and eventually died, like everyone else.

Just as there were three versions of the heresy that denied the full divinity of Christ, so there were a number of heresies that denied the full humanity of Jesus. Apollinarianism is a heresy named after Apollinaris (died 390), bishop of Laodicea in the fourth century. He was a voluminous writer and brilliant defender of the Nicene doctrine of the Trinity. He tried to solve the christological problem of how the person of Jesus can be both divine and human, fully God and fully man. His answer was: in the incarnation the Logos took on the body and soul of the man Jesus, but substituted itself for the human spirit of Jesus, thus assuming a trichotomous view of human being — body, soul, and spirit. He was accused by Nestorius (386-451), patriarch of Constantinople early in the fifth century, of abridging the full humanity of Jesus. The idea that Jesus was fully God but not fully human was condemned as heresy because such teaching violated the logic of salvation. The logic was given its classic formulation by Athanasius: Jesus must become fully what we are so that we might become fully what he is. If in any respect Jesus was lacking in humanity, to that extent salvation was deemed to be less than total.

A second version of the heresy that denied the full humanity of Jesus was monophysitism, a word that comes from the Greek meaning "one nature." Monophysitism sounds like a disease, like mononucleosis. It was worse than a disease because it denied that God assumed human nature in the person of Jesus. Eutyches (380-456), abbot of a monastery near Constantinople in the fifth century, was a monophysite. He came forward teaching that in the incarnation the divine nature overwhelmed and swallowed up the human nature, so that Jesus, though appearing to be human, was really a discarnate God walking around on earth. This illustrates again that what was at stake in all of these ancient christological controversies was the logic of salvation. Monophysitism was condemned by the Council of Chalcedon (451), but monophysite sects were formed in Egypt, Syria, and Armenia and continue to this day in Coptic, Ethiopian, and Armenian churches.

By the "logic of salvation" I have in mind the reasoning implicit in the paradoxical way that Christians speak about Jesus. "Paradoxical" means "contrary to ordinary opinion." It seems contrary to common sense to say that a human being is God. Tom Wright tells of when he was a college chaplain at Worcester College, Oxford. At the beginning of every school year he made a point of seeing every first-year student individually for a few minutes. Many of the students would comment to the chaplain, "You won't be seeing much of me; you see, I don't believe in God." Of course, Tom Wright did not expect atheistic or agnostic students to attend chapel, beautiful as the services of Matins and Vespers can be in the Church of England. He said that he usually responded to these students with a stock answer by saying:

> "Oh, that's interesting. Which God is it you don't believe in?" This used to surprise them; they mostly regarded the word God as univocal, always meaning the same thing. So they would stumble out a few phrases about the god they don't believe in: a being who lived up in the sky, looking down disapprovingly at the world, occasionally intervening to do miracles, sending bad people to hell while allowing good people to share his heaven. Again, I had a stock response for this very common "spy in the sky" theology: "Well, I'm not surprised you don't believe in that God. I don't believe in that God either." At this point the undergraduate would look startled. . . . "No," I would say, "I believe in the God I see revealed in Jesus of Nazareth."[2]

## Why Jesus Is Truly God

People who do not believe in God will be in no position to entertain the idea that Jesus is truly God. They may believe that Jesus existed, even that he was a good man, someone like Mahatma Gandhi (1869-1948). Perhaps they admire his altruistic morality and appreciate parts of the Sermon on the Mount. Others have trouble believing Jesus is God because in their view Jesus does not measure up to their lofty idea of God.

2. Marcus Borg and N. T. Wright, *The Meaning of Jesus* (San Francisco: HarperSanFrancisco, 2000), p. 157.

God is big and Jesus is small by comparison. So we have to ask with Tom Wright, "Where do these people get their knowledge of God, such that Jesus falls far short of sharing his identity?" Wright says that he believes in God in light of Jesus. A formula which I have found useful in decades of classroom teaching Christian Theology 101, over against the ideologies of atheism, agnosticism, or unitarianism, goes like this: "Jesus as subject gives to God as predicate its definitive content and meaning." Luther said "and there is no other God." That is, there is no other God in whom we will put our trust, no other God worthy of our complete loyalty and devotion.

There are other putative divinities, of course. Muslims have their Allah. Hindus have a plethora of gods. New Age people have their earth goddess, Gaia. Here we are simply underscoring that when Christians speak of God, they do so on the basis of the incarnation of God in the person of Jesus Christ. Their reasoning illustrates the logic of salvation. To bridge the chasm between God and the world, between the infinity of God and the finite human world, the Savior must be in good standing on both sides. 1 Tim. 2:5 puts it this way: "There is one God, and there is one mediator between God and men, the man Christ Jesus." If Jesus were merely a man, he would share the predicament of all human beings. He would himself need to be saved; he could not be the Savior. Jesus is the solution and not part of the problem. Likewise, if Jesus were only God, as the docetists claimed, and not fully human, he would have no point of contact with those who need to be saved.

A good mediator is one who can negotiate the differences between two parties. To do that a mediator must be in good standing on both sides. If there is to be reconciliation between two parties at enmity with each other, a go-between is needed. Jesus is the go-between who represents God to humans and humans to God. The logic of salvation affirms that if Jesus were not both God and man, he would be impotent to deal with the religious predicament of human beings in bondage to what Luther called the "unholy trinity" of sin, death, and the devil — enemies of God and oppressors of humanity. Hebrews 9:15 says, "He [Christ] is the mediator of a new covenant, so that those who are called may receive the promised inheritance, since a death has occurred which redeems them from the transgressions under the first covenant."

## The Real Presence of Christ

The Lutheran Reformers and Confessors in the sixteenth century accepted the "high Christology" of the ancient church, but then added a wrinkle of their own. We may call it a Lutheran innovation,[3] going beyond what the Roman Catholic Church had taught throughout the Middle Ages and what the Reformed Churches of John Calvin and Huldrych Zwingli taught. A christological controversy erupted in connection with their respective understandings of the Lord's Supper. Luther taught that at the Lord's Supper the whole Christ is really present, both in his divinity and in his humanity, in, with, and under the elements of bread and wine. Zwingli (1484-1531), the Swiss Reformer, adopted a symbolic view, following Erasmus of Rotterdam, whose theology Luther had seriously disputed in his book *The Bondage of the Will*. Luther understood Zwingli to be saying that the sacraments are only symbolic reminders of the grace of salvation that Christ wrought upon the cross. They are not now the means by which Christ becomes truly and wholly present to impart his gifts of new life and salvation.

When Luther read the words "This is my body," he took them to mean exactly what they say. The little word "is" must be taken literally. Zwingli said, No, "is" means "signifies" here. Christ cannot be present here and now because, as the creed says, he ascended into heaven and sits at the right hand of God. Zwingli took those words literally: Christ in his ascended human body is sitting at God's right hand. Luther interpreted the same words symbolically to refer to the power of God by which Christ can be everywhere present according to his will and promise, at every Lord's Supper no matter how many are taking place at the same time. Lutherans therefore teach that they believe in the "real presence" of Christ and have chided their Reformed cousins for believing in the "real absence" of Christ.

Lutheran and Reformed theologians engaged in a centuries-long controversy on the Lord's Supper, pitching two Latin phrases against

---

3. In defense of Luther's understanding of the real presence of Christ in Holy Communion, sixteenth-century Lutherans taught the doctrine of the *genus majestaticum*, affirming that the attributes of the divine nature of Christ, such as God's ubiquity or omnipresence, are communicated to his human nature.

each other. The Reformed insisted on the proposition that "the finite cannot contain the infinite" — *finitum non capax infiniti*. The Lutheran maxim was the opposite, "the finite is capable of the infinite" — *finitum capax infiniti*, the proof being that it happened in the incarnation: the Word became flesh; God became man. Likewise, in the Lord's Supper the bread and the wine, finite though they be, convey the whole Christ, the one person in both his divine and human natures. The controversy was laden with concepts from medieval scholastic metaphysics, sometimes to the extent that it seemed that the theologians forgot what was at stake. What was at stake is the assurance that Christ descends to meet us bodily at the earthly level of our sinfulness. We do not need to ascend to heaven to meet Christ spiritually at the level of God's holiness in heaven. We are not able to rise above the level of our earth-bound finitude. On account of the incarnation God showed that he is able to meet us deep in human flesh. Salvation is not something we need to reach for beyond space and time. Luther said in effect, "Do not listen to those who say, 'The flesh is good for nothing.' Rather say, 'God without flesh is good for nothing.'" We believe that God meets us in our down-to-earth condition, so there is no need for us to go elsewhere.

Over the centuries Lutheran and Reformed Protestants have not been nice to each other. In recent decades, however, both sides have tried to bury the hatchet through a series of ecumenical dialogues. Thus, the Evangelical Lutheran Church in America has entered into full communion with a number of Reformed churches. Does that put an end to the controversy? Does that mean that Lutherans now accept the symbolical view of Zwingli? Or does it mean that the dialogues convinced the Reformed that the Lutheran realistic view is correct? My best judgment is that some of the differences remain but that they are not necessarily church-dividing, as they would be if the Lutheran agreement with the Reformed reaffirmed Zwingli's error.

My view is that over the long haul good theology drives out bad theology. On the theology of the Lord's Supper I believe the high doctrine that Lutherans have espoused is best for individual believers and congregations. When the Eastern Orthodox weigh in on this dispute concerning eucharistic theology in Western churches, they tend to prefer the Lutheran view to the Reformed. Lutherans in the ecumenical dialogues have not been pressured to abandon their historic emphasis on the real presence. Moreover, Luther's sacramental realism has been vindicated by recent inquiries into the New Testament, especially the writings of Paul and John. It is well to remember that doctrine is not merely a matter of abstract ideas; its pay-off is in terms of concrete practices. Churches with a high sacramental theology do things differently than those with a low symbolical view. Weekly celebration of Holy Communion has more and more become the standard practice in Lutheran congregations. On the other hand, if the Lord's Supper is regarded chiefly as a memorial service, commemorating the ending of Jesus' life, how often do we need to do it? Maybe once a month would be sufficient, maybe not even that.

## A Real Incarnation

We have been explaining how the Christian doctrine of the incarnation developed in the early centuries leading up to the councils of Nicaea and Chalcedon, starting with the unforgettable impression Jesus made on his followers, both before and after Easter. Some years ago a much-publicized book was published in England with the sensational title *The Myth of God Incarnate,* edited by John Hick.[4] The authors of this book used the word "myth" to mean "untrue." Of course, that is not the proper literary meaning of the word. "Myth" is a way of speaking of otherworldly matters in terms of this-worldly symbols.

But the authors of this book intended to say that the incarnation is untrue. It is not real; it did not happen. They called for a "Copernican revolution" in theology. The essence of such a revolution is to put God at the center of the universe of all world religions. The intent is to dislodge Christ from the central position he has held in the old Ptolemaic kind of traditional theology. The doctrine of the incarnation has had a pernicious effect, they say, because it places Christ at the center of the Christian faith. But in these modern times that is like believing in the ancient geocentric cosmology that has the sun revolving around the earth. In their Copernican revolution we must start with God at the center of the

4. John Hick, ed., *The Myth of God Incarnate* (Philadelphia: Westminster Press, 1977).

universe and not with Christ. They start with the definition of God as infinite. God's infinity renders him by definition metaphysically incapable of becoming finite. God is infinite; a human being is finite. The finite is incapable of the infinite. *Finitum non capax infiniti.* In other words, their God would not be caught dead in a human being. God is impassible; he cannot suffer; he cannot bleed. Jesus suffered and bled; ergo, he cannot be God. God is immortal; a human being is mortal. Jesus died; ergo, he cannot be God. God is in heaven; humans are on earth. Heaven and earth are polar opposite; they cannot meet. A real incarnation of God is ontologically impossible for these "Myth of God" theologians.

The attack on the doctrine of the incarnation did not stop with these British theologians. Tom Driver, emeritus professor of theology at Union Theological Seminary in New York, coined the term "christofascism" to ridicule the idea of placing Christ at the center of life and history. Christofascists, he says, are christodolaters. His book *Christ in a Changing World*[5] states that it is high time to get rid of the scandal of particularity. We must get rid of the notion that God revealed himself in Jesus once for all, for all time and for all people. This leads us to the question of the next chapter, "Is Jesus Unique — The One and Only Way of Salvation?"

## Questions for Discussion

1. The creeds of the early church took great pains to confess that the person of Jesus Christ is fully human and fully divine. Why were the church fathers so vigilant against abbreviating Jesus' humanity or his divinity in any respect whatsoever?

2. Contemporary New Testament theologians debate whether or not Jesus understood himself to be the Messiah. Does it matter to the Christian faith one way or another?

3. This chapter uses the term "the logic of salvation." That is the literal meaning of the term "soteriology." Why are Christology and soteriology so closely interrelated in the Christian doctrine of salvation?

5. Tom Driver, *Christ in a Changing World* (New York: The Crossroad Publishing Co., 1981).

4. The tension between "low" and "high" Christologies is evident throughout the history of the Christian tradition and even today. Give some examples of the difference between these two types of thinking concerning the identity and meaning of Jesus Christ.

5. If Jesus were not truly God, there would be no need for the doctrine of the Trinity. Is this a true statement? If so, what is the place of Jesus in the doctrine of the triune God?

6. Martin Luther emphasized that Jesus is really present in his body and blood in, with, and under the elements of bread and wine. Huldrych Zwingli disagreed. What was the controversy between Luther and Zwingli all about?

7. Some theologians claim that the incarnation of God in Jesus Christ is a myth. What is the meaning of "myth"? Are there any myths in the Bible? Explain.

# V

# Is Jesus Unique —
# the One and Only Way of Salvation?

The question whether Jesus is unique, the one and only way of salvation, has been of major interest to me for a long time. Preoccupation with this question has led me to write extensively on Christianity among the world's religions and on the Christian mission to the non-evangelized nations.[1] Where I grew up in South Madagascar, a son of Norwegian-American Lutheran missionaries, we lived in a religiously pluralistic milieu. We met French and Malagasy Roman Catholics, Reformed Protestants, Malagasy Lutherans, Muslims, Hindus, Confucianists, and a majority of animists. The small colony of missionary families was a distinct minority.

The Lutheran missionaries went to Madagascar to preach the New Testament gospel of salvation in the name of Jesus Christ, the Lord of the church and Savior of the world. Interactions between Christians and people of other religions took place constantly on a daily basis. When I came to the United States, I thought it odd that most of my college and seminary classmates were not at all interested in other religions. Lo and behold, the situation has changed dramatically since Sep-

---

1. Cf. Carl E. Braaten, *The Flaming Center: A Theology of the Christian Mission* (Philadelphia: Fortress Press, 1977); *The Apostolic Imperative: Nature and Aim of the Church's Mission and Ministry* (Minneapolis: Augsburg Publishing House, 1985); *No Other Gospel: Christianity among the World's Religions* (Philadelphia: Fortress Press, 1998); *That All May Believe: Theology of the Gospel and the Mission of the Church* (Grand Rapids: Eerdmans Publishing Co., 2008).

tember 11, 2001. The awareness of the average American has been raised to a new level. People now realize that the major world religions are no longer foreign; they are right at our doorsteps. Their mosques and temples are in our neighborhoods. Their followers are increasing in surprising numbers. Talk shows debate how Americans ought to relate to people who are different in their beliefs, lifestyles, and dress codes. The question of the relation of Christianity to other religions has never been more timely and important.

## The Pluralistic Theology of Religion

The religions of the world have often been the source of conflict and violence between peoples. Great effort has been made in recent decades to bring representatives of the world's religions to meet face-to-face in dialogue and to promote the cause of peace. Some theologians are saying that for Christians to do their part, they must abandon their traditional belief that Jesus is the Way, the Truth, and the Life for everybody. Such theologians espouse the pluralistic theory of religion, the notion that all religions are equally valid ways of salvation, that all religions lead people to the same glorious end.

The pluralistic theology of religion is very popular among professors of religion in colleges, universities, and divinity schools. The pluralistic theologians of religion readily admit that their view has no footing in the Bible or the classical Christian tradition. Their basic appeal is to the realities of the modern world in which the religions interact with each other as never before.

The idea of pluralism was born in Hinduism. Over 100 years ago the Hindu Reformer Swami Vivekananda (1863-1902) came to the West proclaiming the message that for 2500 years India had already accepted a religious philosophy of pluralism. Hindu pluralism is well illustrated by the famous fable of the elephant and the blind men. Six blind philosophers make an inquiry into the nature of the elephant. One falls against its side and thinks the elephant is like a wall. A second feels the tusk and thinks the elephant is like a spear. For the others, the trunk is like a snake, the leg is like a tree, the ear is like a fan, and finally, "the swinging tail is like a rope." Each philosopher thinks that his particular experience of the elephant represents *the* truth. Similarly, each of the great world religions thinks its experience of the mystery of ultimate reality is the truth. Along comes the superior wisdom of Hinduism teaching that each of the religions is one-sided and mistaken in its belief that its partial perspective is the whole truth, that its relative grasp of reality is absolute. The pluralistic theory of religions is at home in Hinduism. What is novel is that some Christian theologians are trying to give it a home in Christianity. Christian doctrines and practices would need to be radically revised to provide hospitality to the pluralistic hypothesis.

There is nothing new about religious pluralism as such. Christianity originated when the world was teeming with a great variety of Jewish, Greek, Roman, and Oriental religions. The tiny Christian movement started as a sect within Judaism and had to struggle to establish its own identity and viability in the ancient world. At first the Christian faith was attacked by Jews as a heresy, persecuted by Romans as a seditious movement, ridiculed by Hellenistic philosophers as a foolish myth, and given a run for its money by the popular cults and mystery religions. There is nothing new about Christians being surrounded and often outnumbered by people of other religious persuasions. What is new, however, at least among Christian theologians, is the claim that all religions are equally valid as ways of salvation.

The idea that all religions are equal is the peculiar attraction of Baha'i, a religion founded in Iran in 1863 by Baha'u'llah (1817-1892). The belief that all religions point to the same ultimate reality is architecturally enshrined in a beautiful Baha'i temple in Wilmette, a Chicago suburb. It is built with nine porticoes, each dedicated to the prophet of one of the world's religions. The porticoes provide access via nine aisles converging on a single central altar, which symbolizes the quintessential unity to which the various religions point. It does not matter which portico one enters or down which aisle one goes, all lead to the same place. This symbolizes the pluralistic model; it is the essence of the Baha'i synthesis of the religions. It was an idea waiting to be born, because if it is true and all religions wake up to it, that could put an end to the wars of religion and constitute a major thrust toward world peace.

The pluralistic theologians speak the language of tolerance and generosity toward all religions. They reserve their intolerance for their fellow Christians and theologians who are unwilling to take the same journey from the exclusive gospel of Jesus Christ to an egalitarian pluralism in which all religions offer something equally good and true to their devotees. Evangelical Christians are pitied or excoriated for wallowing in ignorance, prejudice, intolerance, narrow-mindedness, and dogmatism. I do not believe such epithets fit all those who refuse to march down one of the aisles to the high altar dedicated to an anonymous deity at the center of the temple.

A correlation exists between the rise and flourishing of the pluralistic theory of religion and the collapse of world evangelization and world missions in the mainline denominations. Why evangelize, if all peoples are equally blessed by the same God at work to save through the great diversity of religious myths and rituals? How many missionary volunteers could be recruited on the basis of a pluralistic system of beliefs? At best we might expect people to volunteer for interreligious dialogue for the sake of the cross-fertilization of ideas, and if they go overseas, they are sure to have a round-trip ticket in their pocket.

## The Exclusive Claim of the Gospel

Is there a better scenario to guide our thinking? I will begin with a passage from Paul's letter to the Galatians:

> I am astonished that you are so quickly deserting the one who called you in the grace of Christ and are turning to a different gospel — not that there is another gospel, but there are some who are confusing you and want to pervert the gospel of Christ. But even if we or an angel from heaven should proclaim to you a gospel contrary to what we proclaimed to you, let that one be accursed! As I have said before, so now I repeat, if anyone proclaims to you a gospel contrary to what you received, let that one be accursed! (1:6-9)

And another familiar passage from Acts:

This Jesus is the stone that was rejected by you, the builders; it has become the cornerstone. There is salvation in no one else, for there is no other name under heaven given among mortals by which we must be saved. (4:12)

The latter passage is the *locus classicus* that underscores the exclusive claim of the gospel concerning salvation through Jesus' name and by his authority. The exclusivity of the gospel is based on the "one and only" designations of Jesus in the New Testament. He is the only begotten Son of God; he is the one and only Savior of the world. The question is whether the exclusive role of Christ in God's plan of salvation is part of the kernel of the gospel or so much husk than can be stripped away to accommodate many ways of salvation. The pluralistic theologians dismiss the "one and only" statements of New Testament Christianity as due to the narrow cultural perspective of primitive times. What they fail to recognize is that such statements were in fact countercultural in the first century, a scandal to Jews and foolishness to Greeks. The first missionaries like Paul and Barnabas who crisscrossed the pagan world witnessing to Christ must have been narrow-minded, according to the pluralistic theologians. Any fair reading of Paul's sermons will reach the conclusion that he believed, along with the other apostles, that God's act of salvation is mediated exclusively through Christ. One Savior who died on the cross and was raised from the dead was proclaimed as the hope of the whole world.

## General and Special Revelation

Yet when Paul encountered people of other religions, he readily acknowledged that they knew something about God. God had revealed something of himself to all the nations. In Paul's words, "He has not left himself without a witness in doing good" (Acts 14:17). Paul concedes something about morality: these pagan worshippers knew something about doing good. When Paul met the Epicurean and Stoic philosophers in Athens, he announced,

Athenians, I see how extremely religious you are in every way. For as I went through the city and looked carefully at the objects of your worship, I found an altar with the inscription, "To an unknown God." What therefore you worship as unknown, this I proclaim to you. The God who made the world and everything in it, he who is lord of heaven and earth, does not live in shrines made by human hands, nor is he served by human hands, as though he needed anything, since he himself gives to all mortals life and breath and all things. From one ancestor he made all nations to inhabit the whole earth, and he allotted the times of their existence and the boundaries of the places where they would live, so that they would search for God and perhaps grope for him and find him — though he indeed is not far from each one of us. For "in him we live, and move, and have our being," as even some of your own poets have said. (Acts 17:22-28)

We may call this general revelation or natural theology. Paul is saying that there is such a thing as universal revelation. In Romans 1 Paul says: "For what can be known about God is plain to them, because God has shown it to them. Ever since the creation of the world, the eternal power and divine nature, invisible though they are, have been understood and seen through the things he has made." Such general revelation takes place apart from the Bible and the church. When missionaries such as my father and mother arrived in Madagascar, they brought the Bible, preached the gospel, and planted the church, but they found that God was already there. The Malagasy natives called him Zanahary. He was the high power that created everything that exists.

Taking into account the experiences and testimonies of missionaries from Paul's day to our own, I think we have lots of evidence to support the idea of two kinds of revelation, general and special. The idea of general revelation maintains that in creating the world, God has left his imprint on all things in the way he made them. We are created in the image of God, whether we believe in God or not. God is universally revealing something of the eternal power and glory of his unfathomable mystery among all peoples, nations, religions, and cultures. The very fact of religion is a sign that people are responding in some way to God's revelation.

They may not get it right, because their minds have been darkened by sin and superstition. This general revelation is a broad highway that runs through all the religions of humankind.

The purpose of general revelation is to prepare for the preaching of the gospel, the biblical account of God's self-revelation in salvation history. This second type of revelation is a special blue-ribbon action of God that happens exclusively through Christ and his Spirit at work through the church and its evangelistic mission to the nations. This action does not happen equally everywhere in the world; it does not happen in other religions that do not confess Christ. It happens by means of a particular sequence of historical events that begins with the call of Abraham, moves forward in history with the election of Israel to be the chosen people of God, the birth of the Messiah, the death and resurrection of Jesus, the outpouring of the Spirit, the commissioning of the apostles, the spreading of the gospel, and the planting of churches on every continent and in every nation until the Lord returns in glory at the close of the age. This narrow road is the way of salvation in the name that is above every name, the name of Jesus.

## Interreligious Dialogue

The pluralistic model, though seemingly very generous in its attitudes to other religions, gives away the core of the gospel. It substitutes dialogue for evangelism. The pluralists do not believe in converting people from other religions to faith in Christ. They say that the purpose of the Christian mission is to make Hindus better Hindus, Buddhists better Buddhists, Muslims better Muslims, and so forth. They do not believe Christians have any business trying to convert any of these to the Christian faith.

There is a time and a place for both dialogue and evangelization. It is much better for the religions to be in dialogue than to be at war, to be talking rather than killing. But commitment to dialogue should not be a substitute for witnessing to the faith. The Great Commission of Christ is an irrevocable call to evangelize the nations, to teach and to baptize, to preach the gospel and plant new churches. A Christ-centered evangelism should drive us to meet people of other religions in conversation and dialogue. The purposes of dialogue and evangelism are not the same. We should promote dialogue all around the world to increase mutual understanding, reduce tensions, eliminate caricatures born out of ignorance, fear, and prejudice, so that conflicts between the religions may be avoided and removed. These are worthy goals for people of all religions.

We agree with the pluralists that interreligious dialogue is both important and necessary. Our controversy with the pluralists is not about dialogue but about the nature of the gospel. Proclaiming the gospel calls for a change of loyalty, repentance, and faith. It is an occasion for rejoicing when persons of other religions come to faith in Jesus Christ. At the Lutheran School of Theology I had a Chinese doctoral student from Hong Kong. She told how she was raised a devout Buddhist and that, upon hearing the testimony of a missionary, came to faith in Jesus and was baptized. She said she experienced the shock of her life when she came to America and learned that some Christian theologians were implying that she had made a mistake. She should have remained a Buddhist and tried to become a better Buddhist. But, she said, she found no forgiveness of sins, no peace of mind, and no hope of eternal salvation in Buddhism, exactly what she found in becoming a Christian. This young missionary convert is not a friend of the pluralistic theology of the religions.

The theological error of the pluralists is to drive a wedge between God and Christ. They demand theocentricity at the expense of Christocentricity. That makes sense to them, because they believe that Jesus was a mere man. They reject the high Christology of the creeds of orthodox Christianity. Christology must be decreased, because it causes offense when people sit around a table with people of other faiths and discuss religion. The apostle Paul knew about that; he admitted that talk about the crucified and risen Christ is a scandal and a stumbling block. The temptation is great to find common ground with people of all religions. The pluralistic theologians believe that God unites and Christ divides. So for the sake of interreligious dialogue Christ must be the sacrificial lamb; Christ must decrease so that God might increase. When that happens the doctrine of the Trinity collapses. Then we end up with a unitarian concept of God and an ebionite understanding of Jesus. If one does not think like a trinitarian, one will think like a unitarian, and if one thinks like a unitarian, Jesus will not be viewed as the One the New Testament says he is.

John Hick, one of the pluralists, says that we can still be Christian in this post-Copernican age. We can still chant our liturgies, say our prayers, and speak of Jesus *as if* he were God for us, so long as all of this is only metaphorical poetry and not ontological prose. John Hick says, "When I confess as a Christian that Jesus is the Savior of the world," this should be understood as hyperbole of the heart. It's like saying, "My Helen is the sweetest girl in the world," knowing full well that others may have a different taste.[2]

Interreligious dialogue cannot flourish when Christian theologians soft-pedal the great truths of the Triune God and the divinity of Christ. The idea that the religions should set aside their differences because they all supposedly point to the same ultimate reality disregards the fact that religions do actually disagree about the nature of that ultimate divine reality. It is simply not the case that they mean the same thing, though using different words and symbols. The religions should not be expected to abandon their respective truth-claims as a condition of dialogue. Christians who enter into dialogue with people of other faiths do not become better dialogue partners by presenting the Christian faith at a bargain rate. They know that they enter a dialogue with the command of Jesus to love their neighbors as God so loved them. Christians do not need to agree with others to love them. The *agape*-love of God reaches out to embrace those who are different. The profound Christian idea of love is grounded, not in some universal moral principle common to all religions, but in the very being of God, who revealed himself as love, as a communion of three interrelated persons who reciprocally love each other. The idea of a loving God is enacted in the concrete history of Jesus, in his life, death, and resurrection.

## No Salvation Outside Christ

If we say that all salvation is mediated solely through Christ and on his account, everything depends on what is meant by salvation. All religions claim to experience salvation of some kind, but not all mean the same

2. John Hick, "Christ's Uniqueness," *Reform*, 1974, p. 18.

thing by salvation. There is no such thing as generic salvation. The Christian gospel does not promise any old kind of salvation. New Testament Christianity offers a specific salvation in the name of the crucified and risen Lord Jesus Christ. Salvation may mean illumination. That is what the Buddha promises. Salvation may mean unification. That is what Sun Myung Moon, the founder of the Unification Church, promises. Salvation may mean to be blessed by ancestors. That is what the indigenous religions in Africa promise. Salvation may mean immortality of the soul. That is the promise of Hellenistic religion. Salvation may mean liberation from class domination. That is what Marxism promises. Salvation may mean authentic existence. That is what the existentialist philosophers dreamed up. Salvation may mean holistic development. That is what New Age spirituality promises. The point is that not all promises of salvation amount to the same thing.

The pluralists who teach that all religions are ways of salvation fear that so great a stress on the uniqueness of Christ allows no chance for non-Christians to be saved. Once my dentist said to me, while my mouth was full of cotton: "I have a theological question. My daughter asked my wife, if there are people living in out-of-the-way places who have never heard about Christ, can they be saved?" I drooled out some words to the effect that it is a huge question to which there is no satisfactory answer. I would rather live with this unsatisfactory answer than with the unsatisfactory answer of the pluralists who claim to know more than they really do.

We know from the Bible that our Savior God "desires all people to be saved and to come to the knowledge of the truth" (1 Tim. 2:4). We also know that "God was in Christ reconciling the world unto himself" (2 Cor. 5:19). Lutherans do not believe in a limited atonement, as Calvinists do. Lutherans do not believe in a double predestination,[3] the idea that God

---

3. The *Formula of Concord*, Article 11, rejects the Calvinist idea that "God has predestined certain people to damnation so that they cannot be saved." However, it is something of an embarrassment that Luther taught the doctrine of double predestination in his favorite writing, "The Bondage of the Will," *Luther's Works*, vol. 33, tr. and ed. Philip Watson (Philadelphia: Fortress Press, 1972). Luther says that reason cannot understand why God "saves so few and damns so many" (p. 62). I believe Luther was overstating his defense of the sovereign and majestic will of God in his diatribe against Erasmus the humanist of Rotterdam.

predetermined before the creation of the world who would be saved and who would be damned. Lutherans do believe that all salvation is on account of Christ, that he is the only reconciling Mediator between God and man. Does that mean that Lutherans are universalists, believing that everyone will be saved in the end? Certainly not in the sense of the Universalist Church, which holds the belief that all will be saved in the end because, well, people are just too good to be damned.

The doctrine of original sin affirms that all have sinned and fall short. None is too good to be damned. But, on the other hand, we have God's intervention on the cross of Jesus and his resurrection. That is the start of a whole new ballgame. Christ died for all (2 Cor. 5:14-15), not for half of the human race and certainly not only for Christians. Christ was raised for the justification of the world that God loved so much that he sent his only begotten Son. Some theologians teach that only those who have an explicit faith and make a conscious decision for Christ will be saved. If that were literally true, then all the Old Testament patriarchs and prophets would be lost. Catholic theologians teach that there is no salvation outside the church, and then use their ingenuity to find loopholes, like the idea of invincible ignorance. A person who is ignorant of the gospel of Christ but does the best he can to do the will of God can be saved. "It may be supposed that such persons would have desired Baptism explicitly if they had known its necessity."[4] This kind of salvation is a pretty iffy proposition.

Orthodox Christianity has never promulgated a particular dogma on salvation, as it has on the Triune God and the person of Christ. That does not mean that anything goes. The orthodox consensus is that there is no salvation outside of Christ. Whoever is saved is a recipient of the grace of God offered to sinners on account of Christ. "There is therefore now no condemnation for those who are in Christ Jesus" (Rom. 8:1).

The pluralistic theologians are wrong to believe that religions have within them the power of salvation. More often they display the most damnable power to engage in violence and destruction. Christianity as a system of beliefs and doctrines does not save. Only the living God on account of Christ saves. On account of God's act in Christ there is hope for

---

4. *Catechism of the Catholic Church* (Liguori: Liguori Publications, 1994), §1260.

all those who already believe as well as for all those who do not yet believe. At the same time, the threat of eternal condemnation cannot be taken off the table. We simply do not know how things will turn out in the end. But we do have the knowledge of the things we hope for on account of Christ, on account of the universal meaning of his death and resurrection. Christians have good reason to hope that God will in his eschatological power and wisdom find a way to accomplish his desire that all should be saved, and that finally the distinction between those who *already* believe and those who do *not yet* believe will be overcome. Of course, this is not something we can see with our naked eyes, for "hope that is seen is not hope" (Rom. 8:24). Only the eyes of faith in Christ can see glimmerings of "hope against hope." Karl Barth called this an "impossible possibility." It is possible that unbelief cannot nullify forever what took place on Golgotha.

I will quote a passage from one of my favorite Lutheran theologians, Gustaf Wingren (1910-2000):

> That everyone will be saved is not an assertion of fact that has any biblical support. But it is something one can certainly pray for.... No one has arrived. So, while we are in the process of moving toward the goal, we can pray what we cannot assert. For one thing, the New Testament clearly says that God wants everyone to be saved (I Tim. 2:4). To pray for that which God wants is naturally appropriate to the forward movement.[5]

Meanwhile, for Christ's sake we must never look upon any person as beyond redemption. We must act out our hope of salvation for everyone. To hope and pray and work for what God wants is a good thing. That puts us somewhere in the middle between Calvinist double predestinarianism and Unitarian universalism. The view that I am setting forth finds some support in a long line that starts with Paul's kind of universalism in Colossians and Ephesians (the *ta panta* passages) and includes Irenaeus, Origen, and Gregory of Nyssa in the ancient church and Karl

---

5. Gustaf Wingren, *Credo: The Christian View of Faith and Life* (Minneapolis: Augsburg Publishing House, 1981), p. 183.

Barth, Gustaf Aulén, and Dorothy Sayers in modern theology. Nevertheless, there is no single orthodox view of salvation, because that involves eschatology. Eschatology by definition has to do with the final future of all things, things that lie far beyond our knowledge.

In recent decades various Christian groups have become involved in rather high-level interreligious dialogues, mostly with Jews, Buddhists, Muslims, and Hindus. In reading them I have noticed a pattern: high on the list of dialogue topics is their respective beliefs about God and man, and the corollary of that is the seemingly deliberate avoidance of any talk about Jesus. That is a mistake, because what Christians believe about God has everything to do with the story of Jesus. Jesus is a concrete figure of history, and by contrast the idea of God can be very abstract and nebulous, what John Updike described as an "oblong blur." Besides, these other religions do know something about Jesus; they have their own ideas about Jesus, which need to be examined and corrected.

Christians today are challenged to make sense of their confession of Jesus as God and Savior in the context of the world religions. Our Christian confession of the identity and meaning of Jesus meets a world in which the name of Jesus has already spread to all corners of the world. Most of the religions quite readily revere Jesus as a teacher or prophet, as a spiritual leader or moral example. Jews, Muslims, Hindus, and Buddhists can accept Jesus as one of the prophets, revelations, avatars, or Bodhisattvas. Each of these religions has reserved a special place for Jesus in its hierarchy of sacred names and symbols. When Christians meet their neighbors of other persuasions, then dialogue can proceed on many levels. They share many interests bearing on world peace, human rights, cultural enrichment, religious tolerance, and care for the earth. These are all important issues, but then there is that other special dimension of faith, dealing with the deepest mystery of the world and the meaning of life.

## Christians and Jews

In the dialogue between Christians and Jews today, Christians have come to a new appreciation of the Jewishness of Jesus. While this dialogue is helping Gentile Christians to recover their Hebrew roots, Jewish scholars are displaying a new openness to Jesus as their brother. Jesus of Nazareth is the link between Jews and Christians. Jews come from the same household of faith and are blood brothers and sisters of Jesus. Some of us Gentiles have been adopted into the family of God through our faith in Jesus as the Messiah of Israel, and thus both Jews and Christian Gentiles are sons and daughters of the history of faith beginning with Abraham and Sarah. In our dialogue with Jews, we are reminded that Judaism and Christianity are both messianic religions. Jesus is the bond of union between all Jews and Gentiles who confess faith in *YHWH*, the God whom Jesus addressed as *"Abba."* Yet, there is a separation between Jews and Christians, and their beliefs about Jesus constitute the real point of difference.

For Christians, Jesus is the Messiah. For Jews, the Messiah is still to come. From a Jewish point of view, nothing is final and exclusive about Jesus of Nazareth. Jews continue to pray for the coming of the Messiah. Christians pray to the Messiah who has already come. This messianic reference, therefore, unites and divides Jews and Christians. The separation between Jews and Christians is only temporary, according to Paul. In Romans he says that in the end all the Jews will acknowledge Jesus as the Messiah of Israel. That is an eschatological promise and hope that we may all share.

## Islam, Hinduism, and Buddhism

### Islam

Unlike the literature of Judaism, the sacred book of Islam, the Qur'an, contains explicit references to Jesus. Muslims do not reject Jesus. The Qur'an speaks of Jesus in a favorable light. For Muslims, Jesus is a prophet and messenger of Allah; he is even called a suffering servant of God. The Qur'an declares Jesus the Word and Truth of God, in a special lineage of messengers along with Moses, David, and the prophet Muhammad. Christians and Muslims have a point of dialogue concerning the relation between God and the messenger of God.

For Christians, however, the union between God and Jesus is the root of the doctrine of the Trinity. For Muslims, such a personal union looks like tritheism, belief in three Gods. The Qur'an says: "They are unbelievers who say that God is threefold. No god there is but one God" (4.178). For Christians, too, Jesus is a prophet; but he is more than a prophet because he assumed God's authority, forgave sins, and fulfilled the law and the prophets. On the other hand, the Qur'an even speaks of the resurrection of Jesus from the dead and also contains a reference to Jesus' ascension into heaven. In some sense, Muslims affirm that Jesus is alive, that he was taken up body, soul, and spirit into the life and glory of God in heaven.

### Hinduism

When Christians go to the Far East, they find that the image of Jesus has already made an impact on modern Hinduism. Gandhi was inspired by the message and example of Jesus. He said, "It is this Sermon on the Mount that endeared Jesus to me." He also said, "Although I cannot claim to be a Christian in a confessional sense, still the example of Jesus' suffering is a factor in the make-up of my fundamental belief in non-violence that guides all my worldly and temporary actions."[6] The Christian theologian M. M. Thomas (1916-1996) of Bangalore, India, has said that the image of the historical Jesus must be the starting point of the Christian dialogue with people in India, because it contains the power to motivate people to meet the needs of the poor and the oppressed.

No one has any illusions that it is easy to confess Christ today in India. One problem is the imposition of severe political restrictions on evangelization and conversions from Hinduism to Christianity. Another problem is that traditional Hinduism can incorporate the figure of the Christ into its pantheon of divinities, along with Krishna, Rama, Isvara, and Purusha. Its tolerance is limited by its demand that Christians give up the exclusive claim of the gospel and of Jesus being the one and only Lord and Savior of the world. Jesus may be accepted as a yogi or guru, as

---

6. Quoted by Hans Küng in *Christianity and World Religions* (New York: Doubleday, 1986), p. 282.

one among many, or he may be accepted as one of many avatars, one of many incarnations of the transcendent divine Reality.

Hinduism is a missionary religion. We see young Hindu missionaries selling the Upanishads or the Bhagavad-Gita at our major airports. I met one of them at O'Hare Airport in Chicago, a young lady with blond hair and blue eyes. I struck up a conversation with her. I asked her if she believed in Christ. She said, "Yes, I believe in Krishna and Krishna is Christ." She told me that she had grown up as a Lutheran. But now she found that she could be a Hindu without renouncing her belief in Christ. For her there are many Christs.

## Buddhism

The most advanced interreligious dialogue is between Christians and Buddhists. Many Christian theologians have found among Buddhists a sophisticated openness ready for a mutual conversation concerning the things of the spirit. Buddhists interpret Jesus and his message in light of their own understanding of the Buddha and his teachings. Comparisons and differences can readily be drawn between Christ and Buddha. Just as Jesus is the Christ, the anointed One, so also Gautama (ca. 563-483 B.C.) is the Buddha, the enlightened One. The truth of Buddha's teaching on enlightenment, however, does not depend on its relationship to the historical Gautama in the same way as the Christian message of salvation depends on its connection with the historical person of Jesus. Nevertheless, striking similarities exist between the story of Gautama and the story of Jesus. Both became poor wandering preachers with a message of salvation. Both gathered disciples and taught them in the everyday language of the people by using stories, parables, and proverbs. Both criticized the religious authorities, the scribes and priests of their respective religious communities. Both demanded a change of heart and direction, a total commitment, and no halfway measures. Both saw that people are afflicted by a tendency to care too much for the things of this passing world and to render things absolute that are purely relative. Both saw an inordinate drive in human beings to put themselves first — selfishness, greed, or egoism.

What a sharp contrast, however, between the twisted figure of Jesus hanging on a cross, the price he paid for bringing in the kingdom of God's love, and the smiling Buddha sitting on a lotus blossom, exuding tranquility, harmony, and good humor! The crucified Christ experienced rejection, failure, agony, and dereliction as a result of the supreme sacrifice of love poured out for the world. Here again the cross is the criterion of the chief point of difference between the gospel of Christ and all other systems of salvation.

## Questions for Discussion

1. Some modern theologians assert that all religions are equal as ways of salvation. Is this a statement of belief or a verifiable assertion based on empirical evidences from the scientific study of the religions?

2. Do you think the traditional distinction between general revelation and special revelation helps us understand the relationship between Christianity and other religions?

3. The competition among the world's religions has often led to violence and war. How may interreligious dialogue lead to a more peaceful relation between the religions?

4. What is the chief difference between dialogue and evangelism in terms of what they aim to accomplish?

5. Every religion promises its devotees some kind of "salvation." What is distinctive about the Christian understanding of salvation?

6. Some people believe that some will be saved and some will be damned. Others believe that all people will be saved in the end. Do you think there is any way to know which view is correct? How would you make up your mind whether to accept the idea of particular or universal salvation?

7. How is the relationship between Christianity and Judaism different from its relationship to Hinduism, Buddhism, Islam, and other religions?

# VI

# Why Did Jesus Have to Die on the Cross?

The doctrine of the atonement deals with the saving benefits of Jesus' death on the cross. To "atone" is to reconcile, to make two parties "at one" with each other, hence at-one-ment. Our theological question is by no means easy to answer: "Why did Jesus have to die on a cross to bring about reconciliation between God and humankind in bondage to sin, death, and the devil?" We will begin with a brief reflection on Luther's theology of the cross.

## Luther's Theology of the Cross

Luther's theology of the cross was rediscovered in the twentieth century. For a long time it had been ignored, even among Lutherans. Three German theologians have written groundbreaking works that expound Luther's theology of the cross: Walther von Loewenich, Jürgen Moltmann, and Eberhard Jüngel.[1] Lutheran theology will never be the same on account of the influence of these writings. I would go further and predict that Luther's theology of the cross will eventually have a great impact on

---

1. Walther von Loewenich, *Luther's Theology of the Cross* (Minneapolis: Augsburg Publishing House, 1982); Jürgen Moltmann, *The Crucified God* (New York: Harper & Row, 1974); Eberhard Jüngel, *God as the Mystery of the World* (Grand Rapids: Eerdmans Publishing Co., 1983).

theologians, not only in Europe and America, but also in Africa, Asia, and Latin America.

There are, of course, some images of Luther that we would like to forget — for example, the one that has Luther calling upon the German nobility to put down the revolt of the peasants. Luther cried out, "Stab, slay, and smite" the murderous peasants who were fomenting an armed rebellion. Then there's the Luther who fueled anti-Jewish sentiments among the German people, urging the authorities to take action against Jews, to burn their synagogues, raze their homes, seize their prayerbooks, and expel them from the country. The Luther who split the church called the Pope the anti-Christ and other nasty names. Lutheran churches, which bear the name "Lutheran" against the explicit will of Martin Luther, have officially condemned such words and actions of their namesake and apologized to the groups he offended. However, these awful negatives do not nullify the faith that fired Luther's soul and made him one of the great witnesses to Christ in the history of Christianity.

One year after Luther posted his ninety-five theses on the door of the castle church in Wittenberg, he was invited to explain his controversial ideas to the monks of the Augustinian monastery in Heidelberg. This he did, and the result is called the Heidelberg Disputation of 1518.[2] In his lectures Luther set out to revolutionize theology, to turn the theology of his day upside down. Anders Nygren (1890-1978) has called it "Luther's Copernican Revolution."[3] Luther declared that the only theology of any real value is based on the crucified Christ. He sharply distinguished his proposal for a "theology of the cross" from a "theology of glory." Only the theology of the cross leads to the true knowledge of God. The cross is the criterion of all Christian thought and life. Luther said that the only person who deserves to be called a Christian theologian is one who sees the things of God through the suffering and death of Christ. A theologian of the cross sees God in the crucified Christ. In contrast, a theologian of glory seeks to deal with God apart from Christ. We see examples of this in theologies that are heavily oriented to the concept of God in Greek

2. See Gerhard O. Forde, *On Being a Theologian of the Cross: Reflections on Luther's Heidelberg Disputation, 1518* (Grand Rapids: Eerdmans Publishing Co., 1997).

3. Anders Nygren, *Agape and Eros* (Philadelphia: The Westminster Press, 1953), pp. 681ff.

metaphysics, Oriental mysticism, or humanistic morality. Theologians of glory look away in shame from the God hidden in the suffering and death of Jesus on the cross. They want a healthy theology of glory, something to be proud of in nice academic circles.

Almost every year I attend the annual meeting of the American Academy of Religion and the Society of Biblical Literature. There one can learn what professional academics are saying about God and religion. There the theology of glory is in full bloom; the theology of the cross is hidden in the shadows. Our contemporary situation is not that different from what Luther encountered in late medieval scholastic theology. Lots of highfalutin' talk goes on about the glorious God of the universe, but embarrassment prevails when it comes to speaking about Jesus, the humiliated God on the cross. Scholars enjoy talking about the power, wisdom, and glory of God expressed in nature, history, and the soul, developing uplifting theories by which to ascend to God transcendent.

The theology of the cross goes in a completely opposite direction and seeks to learn of God in what the world regards as foolishness and powerlessness, symbolized by the cross. For Luther the God who is really God can be encountered only in the suffering and death of Jesus on the cross, and nowhere else. To meet God and to know God in the cross of Christ means that I myself must be crucified with Christ and that my pride and egoism must be put to death. I must let my ego be nailed to the cross of Jesus. Jesus did not die for himself; he died for you and me that we might find life and have it abundantly. The spectators on the hill outside the gate could not see God hidden in the cross and suffering of Jesus. To meet God in the cross of Christ is to die to ourselves and to die with Christ. Then we will have ears to hear the message of new life in the gospel of Easter, the resurrection of Jesus from the dead.

Luther was serious in saying that the theology of the cross gives us a new concept of God as the crucified Christ. For Luther Christians must not try to think of God and God's attributes without thinking of the crucified Christ as true God. To know Christ is to know God hidden in the suffering of Jesus who exists in solidarity with the sufferings of all people in the world.

Luther used the image of a scale. Unless God puts his weight on one side of the scale, we will sink to the bottom.

If it is not true that God died for us, but only a man died, we are lost. But if God's death lies in the opposite scale, then his side goes down and we go up like an empty pan. . . . But, of course, he could never have sat in the pan unless he had become human like us, so that it could be said: God died, God suffered, God bled. According to his nature God cannot die, but since God and man are united in the one person of Jesus, it is correct to talk about God's death when that man dies who is one person with God.[4]

We hear the same idea in a Lutheran hymn: "O great distress! God himself lies dead. On the cross he died, and by doing this, he has won for us the realm of heaven."[5]

What then have we learned from Luther? (1) The meaning of the word "God" is determined by its reference to the person of Jesus. (2) When Christians think about God in connection with Jesus, it must be remembered that this person was crucified, so that God must henceforth be encountered in the cross of Jesus Christ. (3) The death of Jesus was not an event that affected only his humanity, but also his divinity. Hence it is necessary to say, from a Christian point of view, that God died on the cross and not only a human being. This brings God's life and Jesus' death into the same frame of reference. In a down-to-earth practical sense, this means that when we pray to God and speak about God, we need not think profound metaphysical thoughts but rather focus on the humiliated man on the cross, the One who suffered, bled, and died for us. There is no other God worth the bother. That is Luther's theology of the cross in a nutshell.

Dietrich Bonhoeffer (1906-1945) was one of the few modern theologians who understood Luther's theology of the cross. One of his often quoted statements is: "God allows himself to be edged out of the world and onto the cross. God is weak and powerless in the world, and that is exactly the way, the only way, in which he can be with us and help us."[6]

---

4. Cited in the *Formula of Concord*, Solid Declaration, Article VII, The Person of Christ, *The Book of Concord* (Tappert Edition; Philadelphia: Fortress Press), p. 599.

5. This is a translation of the German hymn, *"O Traurigkeit, O Herzeleid,"* by Johann von Rist (1607-1667).

6. Dietrich Bonhoeffer, *Letters and Papers from Prison,* ed. Eberhard Bethge, tr. Reginald H. Fuller (New York: The Macmillan Co., 1953), pp. 219-20.

Another modern Lutheran who grasped Luther's idea is the Japanese Lutheran theologian, Kazoh Kitamori (1916-1998), who wrote one of the most interesting books on Luther, entitled *Theology of the Pain of God.*[7] It presents an interpretation of Luther's theology of the cross in correlation with the profound Japanese experience of suffering.[8]

Luther's theology of the cross holds the key not only to his idea of the crucified God, but also to the meaning of human existence. The crucified God tips the balance in favor of the freedom of the believer saved by God's grace apart from the works of the law and apart from the achievements of reason. Being good does not do much for salvation and being smart even less. We are morally not good enough and intellectually too dumb to have our efforts count for much in the eyes of God. Works-righteousness and mystical or scientific knowledge are useless as ways of salvation. For Luther the theology of the cross is a path to radical freedom born of the gospel. He said, "A Christian is a perfectly free lord of all, subject to none." At the same time, "A Christian is a perfectly dutiful servant of all, subject to all."[9]

Faith means freedom because it gets sinners off the hook of always trying to attain the righteousness of God by their own reason and strength. The cross is God's way of shattering the way of works to make way for faith, which allows us to live life to the hilt without fear of rejection and damnation. Once Luther wrote to his friend Philip who was sweating over whether he should do this or do that. He felt he was damned if he did and damned if he didn't. We have all been at the crossroads where there are no good choices. We have to choose between the lesser of two evils. Then Luther uttered these audacious words: *"pecca fortiter."* The two Latin words mean "sin boldly." Sometimes this is good advice. Do not be paralyzed by fear that you might make a mistake. "God

---

7. Richmond: John Knox Press, 1965.

8. When I was a visiting professor at the Lutheran Seminary in Tokyo in 1974 I had the good fortune of spending several hours in theological conversation with this great Japanese scholar, discussing, among other things, his idea of the pain of God. He was especially concerned to distinguish his idea from the ancient heresy condemned as patripassianism, a charge that some of his critics made against his book on Luther.

9. Martin Luther, *A Treatise on Christian Liberty* (Philadelphia: Muhlenberg Press, 1943), p. 5.

does not save people who are only fictitious sinners." Make a courageous decision and be prepared to accept God's forgiveness. After uttering the words "sin boldly," Luther added, "But believe and rejoice in Christ even more boldly, for he is victorious over sin, death, and the world."[10]

Luther inherited a theological tradition that offered a number of speculative theories on the atonement. Why did Jesus have to die on the cross? How did the death of Jesus bring about reconciliation between God and the world? St. Anselm of Canterbury (1033-1109) wrote a book on the atonement whose title asks the question *Cur Deus Homo?* In translation Anselm is asking "Why the God-Man?" Why did God become a human being? I will delineate four traditional theories or scenarios that try to explain what the death of Jesus was all about and then end by offering an interpretation that does not contradict but provides an additional insight into the meaning of the death of Jesus.

## The Ransom Theory of the Atonement

Some theologians of the ancient church latched on to several Bible verses that speak of Jesus giving his life as a ransom. This is called the ransom theory of the atonement. Matthew 20:28 says: "The Son of man came not to be served but to serve, and to give his life as a ransom for many." 1 Timothy 2:5-6 says: "For there is one God, and there is one mediator between God and men, the man Christ Jesus, who gave himself as a ransom for all." The ransom view originated in the early church, particularly in the work of Origen of Alexandria (ca. 185-254) and was part of church teaching for the next one thousand years. The question was bound to be asked, though, to whom was the ransom paid? Some answered that the death of Jesus was a ransom paid to the devil to liberate sinners from bondage. The theory was that God allowed the devil to hold sinners captive as just punishment for their sin. As long as the devil held only sinners in bondage, he remained within his rights. But he exceeded his authority when he attacked Christ. The devil was tricked. Because Christ hid his divinity un-

---

10. Martin Luther, "Letter to Philip Melanchthon," in *Luther's Works,* vol. 48, ed. and tr. Gottfried G. Krodel (Philadelphia: Fortress Press, 1963), p. 282.

der his humanity, the devil did not realize that he was attacking the sinless Son of God. Gregory of Nyssa (ca. 335-394) likened Christ to the bait on a fishhook; Augustine likened Christ to the bait in a mousetrap. So why did God become man? The answer of these church fathers was that, in the cosmic struggle between the forces of good and evil, God became man to gain a victory over the devil, the prince of demons. Christ out of his love and willingness to serve gave himself as a ransom in exchange for the captive human race. The devil gladly accepted the ransom, but bit off more than he could chew. He was deceived and defeated.

## The Satisfaction Theory of the Atonement

The ransom theory of the atonement in its most primitive form did not last. The idea that Christ would be a sacrifice offered to the devil was rejected in subsequent Christian tradition. About a thousand years later another theory came along, worked out by the aforementioned Anselm of Canterbury. This is called the satisfaction theory; it is also referred to as the Latin view or the penal theory of the atonement. It became the dominant view in the Middle Ages and continues to be so in Roman Catholicism and conservative Protestantism. Anselm's view has been virtually elevated to the status of church dogma for Catholics and regarded as biblical doctrine by evangelical Protestants. The Book of Hebrews says in many places that Christ offered himself once for all time for sins. It does not present any speculative theory as to why that was necessary, but Anselm does. His basic idea is that a sacrificial offering is necessary as a payment to satisfy God's justice, which is the granite foundation of the whole spiritual world. Because human beings as sinners have failed to measure up to the demands of God's law, they are deeply in debt to him. To be reconciled to God they must make things square and even. They must satisfy God. But this they cannot do on account of their sins. So why did God become man? God became a perfect sinless man so that as man he could make the payment on our behalf; he could do it vicariously as our substitute; he could offer himself as the required satisfaction to offset the sins of humanity.

This law-oriented system was conceived by Anselm to rationalize the medieval penitential system of the Roman Catholic Church. Believers go to the priest to confess their sins. The priest decides the appropriate penance commensurate with the seriousness of the sins that a person confesses. So many Hail Marys, so many *Pater Nosters,* etc. Martin Luther railed against the penitential system because it seemed to promise salvation based on good works. He denied that good works can merit forgiveness. It is impossible to accumulate enough meritorious works to earn one's way into God's good grace. It was taught in Luther's time that saints have more merits than they need. There exists a heavenly treasury of merits that sinners can draw on, for a price of course. Certificates of indulgence were sold by John Tetzel (1465-1519) to raise money for the building of St. Peter's Cathedral in Rome. Merits could be bought for one's deceased grandmother to shorten her stay in purgatory. While Lutherans gave up the system of penance, many retained various versions of Anselm's speculation about the merits of Christ in the transaction of salvation. We cannot make satisfaction for our sins, but we do not need to because Christ has made the perfect once-for-all sacrifice by his obedient sufferings and death.

Every religion in every age interprets its beliefs and rituals in categories native to its own cultural setting. The penitential system was meaningful in the feudal society of the Middle Ages. The idea of sacrifice was the chief motif in the theology of the mass practiced in the medieval Roman Catholic Church. Interestingly, the idea of Christ as the perfect once-for-all sacrifice worked wonders in the agrarian society of Madagascar where I grew up. The Malagasy religion was based on the idea that the ancestors required sacrifices of animals, sheep, goats, and cattle, to appease their wrath and make them happy. If bad things were happening in a village, the witch-doctor would make his diagnosis and stipulate whose ancestors needed placating. Usually it would be someone with a large herd of cattle. Hence many animals would be sacrificed and the villagers would feast for days and then return to life as usual. The missionaries preached from the Book of Hebrews that Christ had made the perfect and sufficient sacrifice for all time; no longer were witch-doctors needed to offer animal sacrifices. The witch-doctors naturally did not appreciate that the missionaries were undercutting their religious authority and way of life.

## The Moral Exemplar Theory

Another theory of atonement quite different from Anselm's was the moral exemplar theory, also referred to as the moral influence theory, put forward by Peter Abelard (1079-1142). Its basic idea is that Jesus' life and death are an inspiring moral example of love and obedience. Sinners are moved by Jesus' example to repent of their sins, improve their lives, and become more loving like him. This idea that atonement happens by Jesus setting a good example for others is very subjective and anthropocentric. It became the dominant view among post-Enlightenment liberal Protestants, primarily because the theory works without requiring the divinity of Christ. Jesus Christ is the perfect example, the ideal man, the head of the race, but he is not more than a man. Reconciliation is the result of a process that takes place in us. Nothing needs to be changed objectively from God's side. The only change that is needed lies in our subjective attitudes toward God and our fellow human beings. The idea that God needs to be reconciled to the world is supposedly a misunderstanding due to the primitive notion that God is a God of wrath and justice, that God has a problem with the world. Jesus' death is a demonstration of self-surrendering love that evokes our loving response.

## *Christus Victor:* The Classical View

The doctrine of the atonement was given new life with the publication of a book written by a Swedish professor at the University of Lund. The book's title is *Christus Victor,*[11] and the author is Gustaf Aulén (1879-1977). The American edition came out when I began my studies of theology. It has had an enormous influence. Aulén did not accept any of the three theories we have discussed, the ransom theory, the satisfaction theory, or the moral exemplar theory. He claims that the *Christus Victor* motif is the classical view, anchored in the New Testament, developed by many church fathers, but which then disappeared from sight for a thousand years until it made its comeback in the theology of Luther. The cru-

11. New York: Macmillan, 1967.

cial biblical passage is: "God was in Christ reconciling the world to himself" (2 Cor. 5:19). Its basic idea is that the life of Christ from beginning to end was a dramatic struggle by which God gained a victory over demonic powers that held people in bondage. The work of atonement is accomplished by God himself in Christ. God is the reconciler and the reconciled. The change is not something that takes place subjectively in human beings. Christ has brought about an objective change in God's relationship to the world. God is pictured as in Christ carrying through a victorious conflict against powers of evil which are hostile to his will. The hostile powers that oppress humanity and that need to be overcome are sin, guilt, death, the devil, the law, and the curse. These are the tyrants that Christ defeated.

## Who Crucified Jesus?

None of these theories of the atonement can be regarded as the final dogmatic truth on the subject. Still, a preacher has to have something to preach about salvation. And the business of the theologian is to offer some guidance. I have never been able to swallow any of these speculative theories hook, line, and sinker. They belong to the history of Christian doctrine, which I have studied and taught. I can understand why each of them had some traction and advocates at various times and places. For me they tend to be overly abstract and theoretical, soaring above the concrete details of the passion narrative about Jesus' final days on his way to the cross.

In what follows I intend to share how I have interpreted the doctrine of the atonement. Reinhold Niebuhr (1892-1971) once said that the core of the doctrine is the simple confession that "Jesus died for us." All the theories of the atonement have that in common before they take off into their speculations. A person may be a Christian and not accept any of the speculative theories of the atonement, but it is hard to see how a person can be a Christian without sharing the confession that Jesus was born, lived, died and was raised "for us and our salvation."

Down through the ages, especially during Passion Week, the church has used Isaiah 53 as a template for its meditations on the sufferings and death of Jesus: "He was despised and rejected by men; a man of sorrows, and acquainted with grief; and as one from whom men hide their faces he was despised, and we esteemed him not. Surely he has borne our griefs and carried our sorrows; yet we esteemed him stricken, smitten by God, and afflicted. But he was wounded for our transgressions, he was bruised for our iniquities; upon him was the chastisement that made us whole, and with his stripes we are healed. All we like sheep have gone astray; we have turned everyone to his own way; and the Lord has laid on him the iniquity of us all" (vv. 3-6). These verses do not give us a speculative theory; they give us messianic prophecy that was literally fulfilled in Jesus' encounters with the powers that humiliated him, tortured him, and put him to death.

"Were you there when they crucified my Lord?"[12] No, we were not physically there when they crucified the Lord. Yet, believers in every age have confessed their solidarity with those who killed Jesus. Jesus was caught up in the personal, social, and political transactions that concern every person in the world. There is no escape. Our Sin (i.e., original sin) with a capital "S" and all of our sins with a small "s" caused the death of Jesus. The whole system of human solidarity — every sphere, every office, every group, every job, ever since Adam and Eve — became one huge conspiratorial plot to draw Jesus Christ, the incarnate Mediator, into the network of evil forces and institutions that succeeded in putting him to death. They made him knuckle under, they cut him down to size, and they refused to let him be the exception he was. And he allowed them to do it. Jesus grappled with evil and the sources of evil, and they snapped back at him, bruising, wounding, and slaying him. But he remained obedient to the Father, faithful to the kingdom of God he came to inaugurate.

Jesus' death was a public occurrence. Traditionally during Lent and Holy Week Christians are moved to dwell on their personal and private sins. They search their souls and expose their most inward feelings. But we should remember that Jesus was put to death not only on account of our private sins, but even more especially by our public sins, our universal human complicity in the public forces and institutions that are still doing their degrading and destructive works of evil.

12. *Lutheran Book of Worship* (1978), Hymn no. 92.

The organized religion of the chief priests and the religious leaders of the people conspired to put Jesus to death. Their religious zeal and bigotry exploded into action. They were angry with Jesus. He flaunted the Sabbath, broke the laws of fasting, and ate forbidden fruit, and with unclean people to boot. This same kind of zeal flexes its muscles wherever religion falls into the hands of power-hungry inquisitors. It happened during the Crusades and the Spanish Inquisition, and it happens in all the modern religious wars, Catholics against Protestants, Muslims against Hindus, etc. Many who have called themselves followers of Jesus are not that much different from the chief priests and elders who put Jesus to death.

Graft and greed and bribery put Jesus to death. Money had a hand in it. The people who controlled the concessions around the temple were the same ones who paid off Judas. Blood money put Jesus to death. It is the same blood money that controls our crime syndicates and corporate tycoons and what President Eisenhower called the military-industrial complex.

Corrupt justice put Jesus to death; he was hauled before a kangaroo court, subjected to a juridical farce, facing flunky judges, false witnesses, and concocted charges.

The mob fell in line with the ruling classes, chanting their idiot slogans to heat up the blood in their veins. They wanted to see a crucifixion. Mobs can be programmed to thrive on violence, to sink into sadism, and switch from the hosannas of one weekend to cries of "Crucify him!" the next. Jesus experienced the invectives gushing from the mouths of intoxicated patriots, driven into frenzy by mob spirit and mob action.

The military was there to carry out the will of the ruling oligarchy. Jesus saw the nation drifting toward war, and his heart cried out for Jerusalem. He fell into the hands of the system that makes for wars. The soldiers did their usual thing. They had the weapons, and so they used them. They stripped him, beat him, and pressed thorns into his scalp. They put a purple robe around him and saluted him. They blindfolded him, struck him, and spit in his face. These were the professional soldiers who always fought in the "just wars" waged by Rome as she defended herself on foreign soil.

Jesus performed his ministry in public, exposed to the same kind of evil powers and systems that we all support and to which we contribute our share. He bore our sins. He felt them in his body and spirit. In doing that he exposed them for what they are. He took up the cross and did not turn away from the bitter cup of suffering. In a way we can only stammer to express, his was so total an act of self-surrender, so complete a response to the demands of service, so absolute a loving identification with the plight of all people trapped by those same deadly powers, that somehow it affected God. The suffering and death of Jesus would have accomplished nothing if that were the end and nothing more. But there was something more, and that is why the Easter event follows the events of Good Friday. If there were no resurrection, there would be no atonement, no salvation, no gospel, no word of the cross. Except for the resurrection of Jesus, the crucifixion would be just like another case of an innocent man sent to the gas chamber, certainly unjust and to be deplored, but with not much riding on it.

The story of Easter teaches us that the powers and principalities of this world do not have the last word. We have proof that they will be defeated; they will not win in the end. Evil powers will be put to death; they will be buried in hell. On account of the resurrection the victim of public violence becomes the victor. We are not slaves but free. We are called to live as those who are freed from religious bigotry, free from political graft and greed, from the corrupting of justice, the mob spirit, the military system, and their collective rule over our lives.

But we still live in the same kind of world that put Jesus to death. All those powers at work to kill him are still at work killing people. They have their hooks into all of us. There is no one who escapes unscathed. As Luther said, though saved by grace, we are still sinners all *(simul iustus et peccator).* The risen Christ still bears the marks, the *stigmata,* of his crucified body in solidarity with a sick and dying world. The cross is what happened to Jesus, who embodied the love of God in the midst of a suffering, godless, and hate-filled world. The cross of Jesus represents the depth of God's love for the world. In Jesus' cross God identified himself with the pain of humanity and its experience of God-forsakenness. The cry of Good Friday can still be heard in the cries of people sent in our lifetime to the gas chambers: "My God, my God, why hast thou forsaken me?" (Mark 15:34).

## Christ Our Representative

Luther was right when he said that an exchange occurs on the cross —
from God to us and from us to God. By raising Jesus from the dead, God
delegated Jesus to be both his representative and ours. I have adopted
the concept of representation to interpret the doctrine of atonement. It
does not figure prominently in any of the other theories of the atonement that we spelled out. But for me it has a contemporary ring. We all
need a representative. We live in a litigious age. When we get in any kind
of trouble, we need someone to plead our cause, to stand up for us, to be
our go-between. We live in a representative democracy. We elect people
to represent our interests and get angry when they do not do so. Faith is
an act of electing Jesus — not Mohammed, Krishna, or Buddha — to be
our representative. As our representative Jesus does not replace us.

The satisfaction theory of the atonement speaks of Jesus being our
substitute. In one sense yes, in another sense no. We still have our grief;
we still have our pain. Christ suffered for us, but he did not suffer instead of us. We still have to suffer. Christ died for us, but he did not die
instead of us; we still have to die. He is not our substitute in the sense
that he replaces us. He is qualified by his life, death, and resurrection to
be our representative. He has the right credentials to be the ambassador
of the human race before God. He is our leader; he goes ahead of us to
prepare a place for us in God's eternal future. Jesus' entire life was repre-
senting the good things of God's kingdom: healing power for the sick,
hope for the dying, forgiveness for sinners, amnesty for outcasts, and a
voice for the poor. Who does not need a representative like that?

But Jesus is more than our representative: he is God's representative.
In some theories of the atonement it is made to seem that only humans
have a problem before God, only humans need to be reconciled to God,
that without the work of Christ and his cross, God would get rid of us and
forget about us or damn us to hell. That may very well be true, but the
other side is equally true. God needs to have a representative to plead his
case in an unbelieving age that asks, "If God exists and if God is in
charge, why does he allow innocent people to suffer and die, why does he
allow bad things to happen to good people?" Who can believe in a loving,
omnipotent God in an age of the gas chambers of Dachau and Buchen-

wald, the atomic incineration of Hiroshima and Nagasaki, the Gulags, and the genocides of Rwanda and Darfur. It appears that God is on trial and that our generation is ready to get rid of a God who does not seem to be doing anything to change the world for the better and to use his power to deliver us from evil.

During the last century atheism has risen dramatically in face of the problem of theodicy. The word "theodicy" stems from two Greek words, *theos* and *dikē*, meaning "God" and "justice." God must be justified. In the Lutheran doctrine of justification, all the accent is on the need of sinners to be justified by God. In light of the problem of theodicy, of senseless suffering and meaningless tragedy, God needs to be justified. Jesus' death on the cross is the best Christian answer to the problem of theodicy. Jesus is God's representative because in his person God is suffering with us. God is not elsewhere; he is there on the cross.

We have come full circle back to Luther's idea of the crucified God with which we began these reflections on the atonement. God in Christ shares deeply in the suffering of all humanity. Bonhoeffer said, "Only a suffering God can help."[13] In the ancient church the question was raised, can the Father suffer? Can God experience pain? Patripassianism[14] was condemned as a heresy by the church fathers. Now we would want to qualify that somewhat and ask, would it not be strange if the Father would be totally closed off from the pain and suffering of his Son?

We started out by saying that there is no single doctrine of the atonement in the history of Christian theology. There is no orthodox dogma promulgated by any church council of the Eastern or Western branch of Christianity. No matter which images or metaphors we use to explain and expound the meaning of the simple confession, "Christ died for us," every orthodox theologian and preacher will be sure not to stray beyond the boundaries of the following principles:

1. Only God can atone. Only God can make us one with him. Only God can reckon with the tyrants of sin, guilt, and death.

---

13. Bonhoeffer, *Letters and Papers from Prison*, p. 220.

14. Patripassianism is an ancient Christian heresy whose adherents believed that God the Father was incarnate and suffered.

2. Jesus Christ is the sole Mediator between God and human beings.
3. An adequate understanding of the atonement must take seriously both the justice and the love of God. Love without justice tends to be sentimentality, and justice without love renders salvation impossible.
4. While the atonement centers most profoundly in the cross of Christ, his earthly life and ministry, bracketed between his incarnation and his resurrection, must also be shown to play a part. The whole Christ is involved in bringing about at-one-ment, that is, reconciliation between God and the world.
5. The atonement is a once-for-all act of God in Christ and does not need to be repeated.

## Questions for Discussion

1. What did Luther mean by a "theology of the cross" in distinction from a "theology of glory"? What are the chief attributes of a "theology of the cross"?

2. "Sin boldly" is one of the most famous quotations from the thousands of things that Luther said. Obviously Luther was not telling people to sin. What do you think he meant by such an audacious utterance?

3. Describe and critique the "ransom theory of the atonement." What is its biblical support? Describe and critique the "satisfaction theory of the atonement." It is sometimes also referred to as the "penal theory." What is its biblical support?

4. The "moral exemplar theory of the atonement" is very popular among liberal Protestant preachers. What do you think accounts for its popularity?

5. Who crucified Jesus? The Romans? The Jews? Both of them in a conspiracy? From a theological perspective is it meaningful to confess that all humanity (all of us) played a role in the suffering and death of Jesus? Explain.

6. Because we are all sinners, we need to be reconciled to God. Does God need to be reconciled to us? If not, why not? If so, why? Explain.

7. What is the meaning of theodicy? Why does God allow the innocent to suffer? Why does God let bad things happen to good people?

# VII

# Was Jesus the Founder
# of the Christian Church?

Alfred Loisy (1857-1940), the French Catholic modernist, made the famous statement, "Jesus announced the coming of God's kingdom,
but what we got was the church."[1] The church is not the kingdom of God.
Jesus had a lot to say about the kingdom of God, but not much about the
church.[2] On the other hand, Paul had a lot to say about the church, but
scarcely mentioned the kingdom of God. In the Gospel that bears his
name, Luke the physician tells the story of Jesus in such a way that everything Jesus said and did is oriented to the kingdom of God. In the Acts of
the Apostles, Luke hardly mentions the kingdom. What accounts for the
dramatic shift from the *kingdom* message of Jesus in Luke to the *gospel*
message of Paul and the other apostles in Acts? The answer is Easter, the
resurrection of Jesus. When Jesus preached the kingdom of God, he did
not preach himself. After Easter, when the apostles preached, they did
not preach the kingdom of God, they preached Jesus Christ. On account
of Easter, Jesus' message of the kingdom of God was dramatically transformed into the message of Christ and his church. Adolf von Harnack
formulated the problem succinctly: "Jesus preached the kingdom of God
as good news, but the apostles preached the Lord Jesus Christ."[3]

1. Alfred Loisy, *The Gospel and the Church*, tr. Christopher Home (Philadelphia: Fortress Press, 1976), p. 166.

2. Only twice in the four Gospels is Jesus reported to have used the word "church":
Matt. 16:18 and 18:17.

3. Quoted from Willi Marxsen, *Mark the Evangelist* (Nashville: Abingdon Press, 1969),
p. 145.

What then is the connecting link between the kingdom and the church? How does Jesus' talk about the kingdom relate to the way the apostles talked about the church? When Jesus preached the coming of God's kingdom, the Jews of his time thought they understood what he was saying. He was speaking their language. In the mind of the Jews, Jesus was announcing that the Messiah was coming to establish the kingdom of God. The Messiah and the kingdom go together. To look forward to the coming of the messianic kingdom is to expect that God will overthrow the dominion of Satan and create a new world of lasting righteousness and blessedness. Jesus expected that God would establish the power and glory of his kingdom on earth, as it is in heaven. The prayer Jesus taught his disciples says as much: "thy kingdom come, thy will be done, on earth as it is in heaven."

The Jews got excited when they heard the prophets announce that the Messiah was coming soon to bring in the kingdom. Jesus was not the first one to preach that. There had been others who preceded him and were proved wrong by the ongoing course of events. Why? Because when the kingdom of God comes, everything will change. Things cannot remain the same. God's coming rule is the power to destroy all resistance to his will. He will bring hope to people in desperate need of a new beginning, poor people, outcasts, and sinners. Poor people will have plenty, the hungry will be satisfied, and those who weep will jump for joy. There will be a turnabout of all things when the kingdom comes. Jesus made it clear that God's kingdom will come as his doing, not as a result of people becoming more religious and doing the best they can, nor by military might and political victory. As a messianic Jew Jesus expected that God was coming soon in power and glory to put an end to suffering, misery, poverty, oppression, hunger, and even death.

But something terrible happened. The messianic hopes and expectations of Jesus and his disciples were shattered on the cross. The Roman soldiers killed Jesus, and his disciples fled for cover in the night. Jesus' friends and followers went away from Jerusalem downcast and sad, saying, "We had hoped that he was the one to redeem Israel" (Luke 24:21). They had pinned their hopes on Jesus, believing that he would establish God's rule to make all things right. But things did not come to pass as expected. Jesus died and the hope for the inauguration of God's kingdom was buried along with him. If that had been the end of the story, the church would not have come into being. But it was not the end of the story. With the resurrection of Jesus and with the outpouring of the Holy Spirit at Pentecost something remarkable happened. A few of Jesus' friends interpreted his death and resurrection as the initial breakthrough of the kingdom, as a down payment on the kingdom that Jesus had preached. The reason was that they believed that, when the kingdom comes, even the dead will be made alive. Paul wrote, "But in fact Christ has been raised from the dead, the first fruits of those who have fallen asleep" (1 Cor. 15:20). Thus, the risen Jesus is the down payment, the first fruits, of the in-breaking of the kingdom that founded the church.

There in a nutshell we have it: no Easter, no church! Without the resurrection Jesus would have been just another forgotten messianic pretender whose hopes and prayers for the kingdom went unfulfilled. We often think of Pentecost as the beginning of the church. But Pentecost could not have happened without Easter. This is important to stress because some modern Protestant theologians try to account for the rise of Christian faith without belief in the resurrection of Jesus. Adolf von Harnack, the great German church historian, wrote a popular and very influential book, *What Is Christianity?*, that sold in the millions. Its central thesis was that all the stuff about the cross and resurrection of Jesus was an invention of the apostle Paul. The real essence of Christianity, he averred, is based on the religion and ethics of Jesus, summarized by Harnack as belief in "God the Father and the infinite value of each individual soul."[4] Harnack's thesis has been renewed by the scholars of the "Jesus Seminar": they call for a new Christianity without the cross and resurrection of Jesus.

## Images of the Church

When the church came into being after Easter and Pentecost, it became necessary to speak about it. Before there were theologians offering propositional *definitions* of the church, there were evangelists and apostles

---

4. Adolf von Harnack, *What Is Christianity?*, tr. Thomas Bailey Saunders (New York: Harper & Brothers, 1957), p. 63.

depicting *images* of the church. The main ones were: people of God, body of Christ, and the new creation of the Spirit.

## 1. The People of God

The disciples and apostles of Jesus after Easter saw themselves as the true Israel. This new self-understanding was based on their belief that the Messiah had come, certified by Jesus' resurrection from the dead. The new wine that came on account of Christ burst the old wineskins. The new beliefs and practices of the fledgling Christian community led to new developments that the rabbis could not endorse and that would not be tolerated in the synagogues. One such practice was *baptism* in the name of Jesus. A second was *prayer* in the name of Jesus. And a third was gathering for the breaking of bread, which Paul called the Lord's Supper.

Israel's favorite self-designation was "the people of God." God said to Moses, "I am the Lord. I will deliver you from your bondage in Egypt. I will take you for my people, and I will be your God" (Exod. 6:6). That is a refrain that runs throughout the history of Israel: God made a covenant with Israel, called them his people and set them apart. God made this insignificant little people the center of the world, the focal point of history, bearing the secret of its meaning. God promised the Jews a land and gave it to them. But the history of Israel, according to her own prophets, was a story of failures, betrayals, and loss of faith. It was a story of sin and idolatry. The history of Israel was the preparatory backdrop to the story of renewal in the arrival of God's kingdom in Jesus' life, ministry, death, and resurrection. The church is the new people of God. However, the original people of God — the Jews — still exist. The new Israel does not replace the first Israel. The two peoples — Jews and Christians — will coexist until the end of history, until that time when, as the apostle Paul says, "all Israel will be saved" (Rom. 11:26).

The Christian church as the new people of God comes from all the nations, all races, classes, cultures, and religions. Some are Jews. They are called messianic Jews, or Jews for Jesus. A person can be born a Jew, but a person cannot be born a Christian. To become a Christian a person must be "born again" through faith and baptism. The call for conversion to Christ can never be limited by race, caste, or class, or ethnicity. God gathers the people of the new covenant from every tribe and nation, from every race and religion.

## 2. *The Body of Christ*

The image of the church as "the body of Christ" indicates that just as "no man is an island" so also there is no such thing as an isolated Robinson Crusoe kind of Christian who exists as a private individual. From the start each person is baptized into the body of Christ and becomes one of many co-equal members. Baptism was not a Christian innovation. Jews were doing baptisms before Christians. Jesus himself was baptized by a Jew, John the baptizer. The difference was that Christian baptism was always done in the name of Jesus. Later that formula was expanded to include the Triune name of God — Father, Son, and Holy Spirit. Luther said in the *Small Catechism,* "Without the Word of God the water is merely water and no baptism. But when connected with the Word of God it is a baptism."[5] Sometimes faith comes before baptism, as in the case of adults, and sometimes faith comes after the act of baptism, as in the case of infants. "He who believes and is baptized will be saved; but he who does not believe will be condemned" (Mark 16:16).

Paul uses the image of the body to admonish members of the community to live in unity, harmony, and mutual respect. Though the body is one, it has many members. All members are important. The eye cannot say to the hand, I have no need of you, nor can the hand say to the feet, I have no need of you. If one member suffers, all suffer together. In a long passage in 1 Corinthians Paul drives home the point that the whole church is the body of Christ made up of individual members who are indispensable to each other.

Every body has a head. Christ is the head of the body, the church. The total Christ is the body and the head together. Where Christ is, there is the church, and where the church is, there is Christ. The body is one with many members. What happens when some of the members mess up?

---

5. "The Sacrament of Holy Baptism," *Luther's Small Catechism,* IV, 3.

This happens when heresies are permitted to invade the body and to lead its members astray. Paul was always warning against the false teachers who endanger the unity of the body of Christ. Unity is endangered by preaching a different gospel. Heresy is a difficult topic from the start, because everybody is a heretic in somebody else's eyes. Paul was considered a heretic by his fellow Jews. The early Christians were considered heretical by the Jerusalem synagogue. Christianity was at first regarded as a Nazarene sect and a Jewish heresy. The word "heresy" means to choose for oneself and to deviate from the consensus of the community. A believer who deviated from that consensus became subject to excommunication, exclusion from the fellowship.

### 3. The Temple of the Holy Spirit

The Holy Spirit makes a person a member of the body of Christ. Luther's explanation of the Third Article of *The Apostles' Creed* states: "The Holy Spirit has called me through the Gospel, enlightened me with his gifts, and sanctified and preserved me in true faith, just as he calls, gathers, enlightens, and sanctifies the whole Christian Church on earth and preserves it in union with Jesus Christ in the one true faith."

Paul said to the Christian community in Corinth, "Do you not know that you are God's temple and that God's Spirit dwells in you?" (1 Cor. 3:16). In the Old Testament, but also in pagan religion, God was thought to dwell in temples made of stone. But now God lives in you, the people of God, the body of Christ. You are the living stones of the temple of the Holy Spirit, flesh and blood members of the new community of Christ.

But even such an ennobling idea can be corrupted. Since we have received the Spirit, perhaps we can control the Spirit in our self-interest. The Spirit bestows charisms or spiritual gifts on individuals, such as healing or the ability to perform miracles, speak in tongues, or drive out demons. Paul was not opposed to such gifts of the Spirit, but for him they were not of highest importance: "I thank God that I speak in tongues more than you all; nevertheless, in church I would rather speak five words with my mind, in order to instruct others, than ten thousand words in a tongue" (1 Cor. 14:18-19).

Paul said there are two criteria for recognizing the work of the Spirit: the first is confessing Jesus as Lord;, and the second is serving the community, to edify and build it up for the common good, such as acts of mercy, teaching, and helping others. These criteria proved essential for Luther in his conflict with the people who believed that they were powerfully endowed with the Spirit. He called them "enthusiasts" or *"Schwärmer"* in German. While he was defending his teaching over against Rome, he was attacked from the other side by the radical reformers, led by Thomas Münzer (1490-1525). Münzer was an early follower of Luther, but Luther's ideas were not radical enough for him. Münzer believed he was directly enlightened by the Holy Spirit and thus had a special gift of biblical interpretation. He was able to turn the dead letters of the Bible into living words. Luther could not accept the main idea of the spiritual enthusiasts. They set the revelations they received from the Holy Spirit above the once-for-all revelation of Jesus Christ in the plain texts of the Bible.

For Luther the work of the Holy Spirit is to lead people to the gospel of Christ, not to lure them into fanciful speculations about the future or the end of the world. It is not the function of the Spirit to give us new revelations, new doctrines, new prophecies which supersede the revelation of God in Jesus Christ. According to the Gospel of John, Jesus promised that the Spirit "will bring to remembrance" everything that he had said (John 14:26). The Spirit will not "speak on his own authority" (16:13) but will "glorify Christ" (v. 14). He will take all that the Father has given to his Son and declare it to the Son's followers (v. 15). In a moment of sheer exasperation, Luther once quipped of the enthusiasts that they have "devoured the Holy Spirit feathers and all."[6]

## The Four Pillars of the Early Church

The church that emerged from the apostles, evangelists, and missionaries of the first century developed the means by which it might remain faithful to its origins in the gospel of Jesus Christ and at the same time

---

6. Martin Luther, "Against the Heavenly Prophets in the Matter of Images and Sacraments," *Luther's Works,* ed. Conrad Bergendoff (Philadelphia: Fortress Press, 1958), p. 83.

meet the challenges of every new cultural situation. There were basically four pillars on which the early church was built.

1. The first pillar was the *creed*. The core of the Apostles' Creed was called the "Rule of Faith" and was first used as a baptismal formula. A non-creedal Christianity never existed. The baptismal formula was at first simply in the name of Christ, because the first converts were Jews who already believed in God the Father. Later when Gentiles came into the church the christological formula was expanded into its trinitarian form, such as we have in the Apostles' Creed. When the Arian heresy threatened the church, the fuller trinitarian statements of the Nicene Creed were used at baptism. Subsequently every Christian was baptized into the triune name of God — Father, Son, and Holy Spirit.

2. The second pillar was the *canon*. Certain apostolic writings, Gospels and Epistles, were selected to form the canon of the New Testament. The Church Fathers used the New Testament canon to interpret the Hebrew Scriptures and all subsequent Christian tradition on account of its witness to Christ and the gospel.

3. The third pillar was the *Lord's Supper,* the weekly celebration of the Lord's presence in breaking bread and sharing the cup of wine. The theology of the Eucharist or Holy Communion was not everywhere the same, but the practice of gathering for worship every Sabbath invariably retained the elements of bread and wine.

4. The fourth pillar was the *ministry,* the emerging threefold pattern of *church order* that included bishops, presbyters, and deacons. The Pastoral Epistles make clear that by the end of the first century the church catholic had established a threefold order of ministry. That was embedded in the great tradition of catholic Christianity until unfortunate events occurred in sixteenth-century Germany to disrupt it. Since then many Protestant churches that abandoned the threefold ministry have tried to make a virtue out of a necessity, claiming that they were only restoring the way the church organized itself from the beginning.

These four pillars — creed, canon, cult, and church order — on which the ancient church was built equipped it to distinguish the true faith from false alternatives. There were many who claimed to be heirs of Jesus and the apostles whose teachings were dismissed as heresies by church theologians, bishops, and councils. The threats to the emerging church of catholic orthodoxy came from two sides, Judaism and Gnosticism. All the first Christians were Jews. The dominant form of Judaism was that of the Pharisees, led by the rabbis. It is called rabbinic Judaism. Other forms of Judaism that we read about in the New Testament withered and died — the Zealots, Essenes, and Sadducees. The Zealots were those who wanted to revolt against the Romans and got killed for trying. The Essenes withdrew to the caves and separated themselves from the evil empire. The Sadducees, like the Herodians, played ball with the Roman occupation. The future belonged to the Pharisees. The two religious streams emerging out of Palestine in the first century, Christianity and Judaism, began to define themselves in radical opposition to each other. The poor Jewish Christians found themselves being black-balled by both Gentile Christianity and rabbinic Judaism. The theology of Paul and John won out and shunted the Jewish Christian sects to the sidelines. They had a low Christology. To them Jesus was a mere man, a prophet, yes, but not the Son of God. Eventually they were no longer a challenge to orthodox catholic Christianity, with its four strong pillars of canon, creed, cult, and church order to sustain it.

But a mighty challenge did come from a completely opposite direction, from the world of Hellenistic mystery religions. The pagan religiosity in the Greco-Roman world was syncretistic. Syncretism happens when beliefs and practices from many different religions are mixed together, something like the "New Age" religiosity of today. The name for this syncretistic religiosity is "Gnosticism." When elements from the Bible and Christianity were added to the stew, the result is called "gnostic Christianity." Dan Brown's novel *The Da Vinci Code*[7] gives a pretty good idea of what gnostic Christianity was like.[8] That book is filled with a lot of goofy beliefs from old-fashioned gnostic Christianity. One was that Jesus fathered a baby with Mary Magdalene.

Gnostic Christianity never died. It went underground during the Middle Ages. It has resurfaced in California and other places among the intelligentsia. "Gnosticism" is a word that comes from *gnosis,* which

---

7. Dan Brown, *The Da Vinci Code* (New York: The Doubleday Publishing Group, 2003).

8. See also the truly informative book by Philip J. Lee, *Against the Protestant Gnostics* (New York: Oxford University Press, 1987).

means "knowledge" in Greek. A gnostic is a person who believes that salvation is gained through esoteric knowledge of mysteries hidden from ordinary people. Gnostic Christianity in the ancient church held four basic beliefs: (1) The cosmos, the world, was made of two completely different things, spirit and matter. The upper spiritual reality was created by a good God; the lower material reality was created by a different god, an evil god. (2) A human being is made of two parts, a heavenly soul indwelling a material body. The soul is a divine spark imprisoned within a blob of filthy flesh. (3) Salvation consists in liberating the immortal soul from the dungeon of this mortal body, to leave the inferior world here below for the upper world of celestial paradise. (4) The only thing that Christianity added to this dualistic system of gnostic religion was belief in Christ. Christ came down to earth to bring the saving knowledge or gnosis to the souls lost in material darkness.

When gnostic evangelists spread these beliefs, they made them sound so Christian and Christ-centered that many gullible people swallowed them hook, line, and sinker. In 1945 an Egyptian peasant named Mohammed Ali (not the famous boxer) ventured into some mountains in Egypt to look for natural fertilizer. He found a large earthenware jar which contained a number of leather-bound documents. He brought them home and threw them on a pile of straw ready to use for kindling. Eventually they were rescued and taken to a museum, where scholars translated them from the Coptic language. Up until then we knew about gnostic Christianity only from the polemical writings of orthodox theologians like Irenaeus and Tertullian, who described and rejected the beliefs of Gnosticism as heretical. Recently scholars have had a heyday filling in the gaps of knowledge and have reconstructed a pretty good picture of gnostic Christianity.[9] When John's Gospel says that "the Word became flesh," that became the cardinal Christian principle invoked against Gnosticism. The orthodox fathers said that the flesh is good[10] and that there is nothing the matter with matter. God created matter, and he did not create

9. Nag Hammadi is the site where the gnostic writings, dating back to the second century A.D., were found. The most famous is the *Gospel of Thomas*. See James M. Robinson, *The Nag Hammadi Library* (San Francisco: HarperSanFrancisco, 1988).

10. It should be noted that the New Testament frequently uses the word "flesh" in a negative sense, as opposed to the "spirit."

anything evil. The orthodox fathers affirmed the goodness of the body and believed in the resurrection of the body and in the church as the body of Christ. Salvation is not escape from the body. Sanctification is not a process of becoming spiritual and leaving the body behind.

By the third century orthodox catholic Christianity had silenced its opposition from the Jewish Christians as well as from the gnostic Christians. Under the rule of the Roman emperors, starting with Constantine the Great, eventually Christianity became the only religion with the official stamp of approval. That was a good thing and it was a bad thing. Ambiguity is the word to describe what happened. Every religion wants to win, but when it does, it pays a heavy price. The New Testament Christianity of Jesus and the apostles became Christendom, the ruling state religion of the Holy Roman Empire.

## Back to the Religion of Jesus?

Prophets of the new age declare that the four pillars of traditional Christianity have crumbled. The leaders of the "Jesus Seminar" are prone to say, "good riddance." Instead, they call for a return to the religion of Jesus. They avow that their historical research has liberated Jesus from the scriptural, creedal, and cultic wrappings by which the church smothered his revolutionary teachings about the kingdom of God. The gap between Jesus and the church, they say, is unbridgeable. For them the bridge has collapsed, and that is the belief that Jesus really did rise from the dead. We agree with the fellows of the "Jesus Seminar" to this extent: no Easter, no church. It is not possible to get to the historical church from the historical Jesus without crossing the bridge that led from his death on the cross to his new risen life in the Spirit.

Robert Funk (1926-2005), the head of the "Jesus Seminar," offered a picture of Christianity based on the religion of Jesus apart from the church. Here are some of his proposals to reconstruct Christianity for the new age: (1) Jesus rather than the Bible or the creeds becomes the norm for Christian beliefs and practices.[11] (2) Jesus is one of the great

---

11. Robert Funk, *Honest to Jesus* (San Francisco: HarperSanFrancisco, 1996), p. 301.

sages of history, and his insights should be taken seriously but tested by reference to other seers.[12] (3) We can no longer rest our faith on the faith of Peter or Paul.[13] (4) Jesus himself should not be, must not be, the object of faith. That would be to repeat the idolatry of the first believers.[14] (5) We will have to abandon the doctrine of the blood atonement.[15] (6) We will need to interpret the reports of the resurrection for what they are: our glimpse of what Jesus glimpsed.[16] Christianity today faces an either/or. Either we go back to the religion of Jesus and try to recreate Christianity for the new age on that basis, letting the quest of the historical Jesus lead the way, or we move forward in continuity with the emerging church after Easter, following the trajectory of the early centuries when the four pillars of the orthodox catholic church were erected.

## The Marks of the Church

In the Nicene Creed we confess that "we believe in the one, holy, catholic, and apostolic church." That is admittedly a far cry from Jesus' preaching of the kingdom of God. Jesus performed the coming of God's kingdom by means of his words and deeds, parables and miracles, and especially by dying on the cross and rising from the dead. The church preserved its memory of Jesus by including the four Gospels in the canonical writings of the New Testament. The church never substituted its creedal propositions about Christ and the Trinity for the down-to-earth stories that Jesus told and that the Gospel writers told about him. Christ the icon never replaced Jesus the iconoclast, as charged by the fellows of the "Jesus Seminar." It is true that the Apostles' Creed and the Nicene Creed do not have anything to say about the life and ministry of Jesus of Nazareth between his birth and his death. That is not because the church forgot about him or neglected to preach from the Gospels. Rather, the creedal formulations were made to confront the heresies of the time; they all

12. Funk, *Honest to Jesus*, p. 302.
13. Funk, *Honest to Jesus*, p. 304.
14. Funk, *Honest to Jesus*, p. 305.
15. Funk, *Honest to Jesus*, p. 312.
16. Funk, *Honest to Jesus*, p. 313.

bear the marks of controversy, always clearly defining what Christians believe over against what they do not believe. The confessions were usually accompanied by condemnations.

The four attributes of the church — one, holy, catholic, and apostolic — were forged in the heat of controversy and continue to help Christians to distinguish a true from a false church. When people move to a new city, chances are that they will find a church on every corner in the town square. They need to know how to tell the difference between an authentic church that exists in unbroken continuity with Jesus and the apostles and a modern sect made in the U.S.A., of which there are many. Or perhaps they do not want to join a liberal Protestant denomination that has capitulated to the isms of contemporary culture. The four pillars of catholic Christianity that we discussed earlier — canon, creed, cult, and church order — are under siege in both instances. The aim of real theology in the service of the church is to point to its historic characteristics. The question it poses is: "Does this visible congregation possess the marks of the true church, that is, is it one, holy, catholic, and apostolic?" That is a tall order. How many congregations in American Christianity that we know merit a positive answer? If a newcomer to a town can say, "Yes, this congregation meets the conditions signified by these four classical attributes," that person can in good conscience choose to join the fellowship. But if the answer is "No," then it is the duty of every Christian to decline its warm hospitality.

Still there is a huge problem in an age of denominational pluralism. So many churches not in fellowship with each other claim with equal conviction that they belong to the one, holy, catholic, and apostolic church. They thus lay claim to the same attributes. Martin Luther and the other Reformers stressed their adherence to the creeds of the ancient church, the Apostles' Creed, the Nicene Creed, and the Athanasian Creed, word for word the same as their Roman Catholic adversaries. Luther argued, in effect, that just because you claim that yours is the true church with the traditional marks does not necessarily make it so. That is when Luther and Melanchthon added an additional criterion of the true church: "where the gospel is purely taught and the sacraments are rightly administered."[17] Here the word "purely" means "according to the

---

17. The *Augsburg Confession*, Article 7.

Scriptures" and the word "rightly" means according to the Lord's institution. The Reformed and Anglican Churches followed the Lutheran Reformation in this respect.

For the next four to five hundred years, all the churches quarreled over the question of which is the true church. Every church claimed the same attributes for itself. No church confessed that it failed to preach the gospel purely and to administer the sacraments rightly. No church admitted that the four classical attributes — one, holy, catholic,[18] and apostolic — do not apply to itself. After Vatican II most churches became involved in inter-confessional dialogues with the intent of promoting the ecumenical quest for church unity. They no longer claim that they are the only true church, and that others are false. Not even the Roman Catholic Church confesses today that it is the only true church on earth, though its theologians since Vatican II have debated at length in what sense non-Roman churches are also the church of Jesus Christ. Over two hundred churches belong to the World Council of Churches. That is testimony to the huge success of the modern ecumenical movement. Regrettably, some conservative Lutheran, Reformed, Baptist, and independent churches refuse to participate in the ecumenical quest for church unity, believing that to do so would yoke themselves with those in error. According to its constitution the World Council of Churches is a "fellowship of churches, which confess our Lord Jesus Christ as God and Savior according to the Scriptures and together endeavor to accomplish what they are called to do to the glory of God the Father, the Son and the Holy Spirit." The Unitarians could not sign that statement. They lobbied to change the wording to get rid of the confession of "the Lord Jesus Christ as God and Savior" and the phrase "according to the Scriptures."

The ecumenical movement is an admission that the plurality of divided churches is a scandal and an obstacle that impedes the worldwide Christian mission to the nations. When the early Christians spread the flame of the gospel throughout the world, those whom they sought to convert were impressed with how Christians loved and served each other. Often the power of their love was more persuasive than the truth

---

18. Most Protestant churches surrendered the word "catholic" to the Church of Rome, preferring instead to use the word "universal."

of their doctrines. The modern ecumenical movement began among the missionaries in India who repented of their lack of love and acceptance of each other. With so many separated churches trumpeting the Christian message, which one of them is really credible? If the Christians cannot get their act together, perhaps none of them is trustworthy. How do churches in conflict bring credibility to the gospel?

The four classical attributes of the "one, holy, catholic, and apostolic church" represent not the way the church actually is but the way it ought to be, the way Christ intended his church to become. None of the churches in the sad state of divided Christianity can claim to be perfectly one without divisions, perfectly holy without sinfulness, perfectly catholic without provincialism, perfectly apostolic without error. If the church were already all that it is meant to be, its earthly journey would have come to an end. The church militant is on its way, always in a state of flux and becoming, and at the same time always in need of reform and renewal. Martin Luther wrote a treatise on the one, holy, catholic, and apostolic church in which he constructed a useful list of seven visible distinguishing marks or characteristics:[19]

1. The first mark is the true preaching of the Word of God. This is the external word that is proclaimed in audible words that people can hear, believe, profess, and live. If there is a group of people who regularly gather around the preaching of God's Word, that is a sure sign of a true church.

2. The second mark is the sacrament of baptism. The church of Christ is surely present wherever holy baptism is administered according to Christ's command. It does not even matter much who does the baptizing. A lay person can perform a baptism, provided it is done with the intention to act in behalf of the church.

3. The third mark is the sacrament of the altar. The church is present wherever the sacrament is rightly administered, believed, and received according to Christ's institution. The person who administers the sacrament may not be particularly worthy or holy, but the sacrament is valid nevertheless. The Lord of the church is the host who presides at his Table.

4. The fourth mark is the exercise of the office of the keys — absolu-

---

19. Martin Luther, "On the Councils and the Church," *Luther's Works*, vol. 41 (Philadelphia: Fortress Press, 1966), pp. 148-68.

tion. The church has traditionally practiced both public and private confession and absolution. In many churches the practice of private confession has petered out, and often has given way to pastoral counseling, by all measures an inadequate substitute.

5. The fifth mark is the office of the ministry. Certain persons are called and ordained to preach the word, administer the sacraments, and pronounce absolution in the name of the church.

6. The sixth mark of the church is worship. People are to gather for prayer, praise, and thanksgiving on every Lord's Day. They pray the Lord's Prayer and the Psalms, they confess their faith in the words of the Apostles' Creed, and they sing hymns. Wherever you see this happening, rest assured that the people of God are there.

7. The seventh mark of the church is bearing the cross of Christ — discipleship. The disciples of Christ who adhere to the faith will be a suffering church. The church is built on the blood of the martyrs. Discipleship is related to the word "discipline." Disciples are a disciplined people.

These seven marks of the church serve as a kind of litmus test that any poor soul can apply in a given situation. Does this congregation measure up? If not, look for one that does. The church in every age needs to be reformed and renewed to be faithful to the church founded by the apostles on the foundation of Jesus Christ. The marks and criteria of the true church are gifts that have been handed down to us from the great tradition of orthodox Christianity.

## Questions for Discussion

1. What is the meaning of the "kingdom of God" in the message of Jesus? Is it present or future or both? Is it this-worldly or otherworldly or both?

2. What is the relationship between the kingdom of God and the church? Between the kingdom of God and the world? Between the church and the world?

3. Which of the many images of the church do you find most fitting: the people of God, the body of Christ, the temple of the Holy Spirit, or some other?

4. The early church developed systems of support — canon, creed, worship, ministry — to maintain its identity and faithfulness through the discontinuity of changing times and situations. Do you think the Holy Spirit had something to do with such historical developments? Which of these four channels are constant and which are variable?

5. What were some of the chief differences between Jewish Christians and gnostic Christians in the early church? What do you think of the contemporary "Jews for Jesus" movement? What are some signs that gnostic Christianity still exists?

6. Martin Luther identified seven marks by which to recognize a true church of Christ. Are they all equally important? Try to rank them in their order of importance.

7. The founder of the "Jesus Seminar," Robert Funk, proposed building a new Christianity based on what Jesus actually taught, and not on the beliefs of the apostles Peter, Paul, and John. What do you think are the merits of such a proposal?

# VIII

# What Does Jesus Have to Do with Politics?

W hat did Jesus have to do with the political movements of his time? Was he a revolutionary? He certainly was not a Zealot. The Zealots were guerrilla fighters trying to establish the kingdom of God by forcefully driving the Romans from the land of Israel. Religion and politics for them were one and the same, something like the radical Islamists of today who commit acts of violence in the name of Allah. Jesus was not that kind of revolutionary. He did not believe in violence of any kind. Like many other pacifists, Mahatma Gandhi was inspired by the example of Jesus in founding his nonviolent movement.

## Jesus, Revolution, and Politics

However, Jesus could not escape the political agitations of his period. He was not like an Essene who hid away in a desert cave. He died by crucifixion, the Roman way of executing a political rebel. It was the Romans who put the inscription on his cross, *INRI*, signifying "Jesus of Nazareth, King of the Jews." It would be wrong to claim that Jesus had nothing to do with the political situation of his day. He called Herod a "fox." He spoke about kings who oppress the people and yet want to be called their "benefactors" (Luke 22:25). He projected the kind of image that caused the crowd to want to make him king on the spot. Among his twelve disciples several were probably Zealots. At least one was carrying a weapon when Jesus was arrested in Gethsemane. And the cleansing of the Temple was done with some force. The Zealots hoped for the kingdom of God, exactly the message that Jesus preached. The difference was that for Jesus the kingdom of God would not come in the style of the Zealots, by revolutionary violence. Jesus told his followers not to resist evil and not to draw the sword. He accepted tax collectors among his disciples and friends, people who were doing business with the enemy. No Zealot would be doing that.

Jesus was a unique kind of revolutionary. He expected the kingdom of God to come and put an end to the present world order. He did not propose its violent overthrow, nor did he flee to the wilderness and wait for it to happen. Unlike the Essenes, Jesus took his kind of revolution downtown into the thick of things. That is the meaning of the charge that he was "a glutton and a drunkard, a friend of tax collectors and sinners" (Matt. 11:19). Looking toward a kingdom not of this world, Jesus stayed in the midst of the world unafraid to point out what is wrong. Consider injustice: Jesus said, "Woe to you that are rich!" The glaring gap between the rich and the poor is completely unacceptable. For this reason it is practically impossible for rich people to inherit the kingdom (Luke 18:24-27). That is a hard saying in a capitalistic society. One wealthy individual was told to sell everything and give to the poor. This saying hit Francis of Assisi (1182-1226) so hard that he took it literally, setting an example that many have followed. When later the established church accepted favors from the wealthy class, its theologians said that Jesus did not intend his statements to be taken literally. But the first Christians, according to the Book of Acts, would not agree with that. They founded a community in which the distinctions between rich and poor were abolished; "they had everything in common" (Acts 4:32).

Jesus was not a politician or a political revolutionary but his words and acts were not so neutral as to be beyond the pale of political involvement. The masses wanted to hail him as a political Messiah, and Satan offered him the kingdoms of this world, but Jesus refused the temptation. He said, "My kingdom is not of this world" (John 18:36). This statement belongs within the framework of his apocalyptic eschatology, which prevented his revolution from becoming merely political. Political revolutions tend to be superficial, lacking the eschatological dimension.

Let us examine some concepts implicit in Jesus' apocalyptic eschatology. (1) The first is the concept of *total change*. The new that is coming involves a complete break with the present order. Politics presupposes too much continuity. In apocalyptic thought the great reversal of cosmic proportions will be preluded by catastrophe, chaos, and calamity. (2) The second is the concept of the *demonic*. There are powers and principalities of which political structures and programs are only representative. These demonic powers are like the "isms" that possess people's minds — Nazism, Communism, Fascism, racism, and the like. (3) The third is that present realities are not all they seem to be, but are *signs of the times* pointing beyond themselves. Events have meanings, if only someone can read the signs of the times. That is prophecy. (4) The fourth is that the coming kingdom calls for *radical conversion* on the part of those who hear the message. Jesus said, "You must be perfect, as your heavenly Father is perfect" (Matt. 5:48). (5) The fifth category is unconditional surrender to *absolute love* — love for God and for all others. This makes it impossible to love just those on the right side, or on the left side, or on my side. Jesus' revolutionaries pray for those who persecute them. (6) The sixth category is the *proletarian principle*. The kingdom comes when the blind can see, the lame can walk, the lepers are cleansed, the deaf can hear, the dead come alive, and the poor have good news preached to them. Those at the bottom will be lifted up. (7) The seventh category is the *reversal of roles*. Jesus said, "The last shall be first, and the first shall be last" (Matt. 10:30). Let the one who would be your leader become your servant — a new insight into the ordering of human relations. (8) The eighth category is that when things seem most hopeless, they may be *birth pangs* of the future. The darkest hour may give way to glimmerings of new light. Salvation may come through suffering. The *eschaton* is not death but life. So in spite of all, this is a time to hope. I believe these categories may be helpful in understanding the radicality of Jesus' message of the kingdom of God.

## The Kingdom, the Church, and the World

Jesus expected God to establish the power and glory of his reign in the near future. But we know what happened. The kingdom of God did not come and change the world in a fundamental way, as far as ordinary eyes can see. The promise of Jesus' message that God was coming soon to destroy all resistance to his rule and turn things around was shattered by the power struggles that got him nailed to the cross. The fulfillment did not come to pass as expected. Not long after the crucifixion a few of Jesus' friends projected upon the world an interpretation of his suffering and death in the light of his resurrection that would be heralded as "good news." And thus the church came into being in the power of the Spirit, who convinced the first believers that the crucified and risen Jesus is Christ the King and as such the down payment of the kingdom that he preached. As a consequence many of the first generation Christians believed that Jesus would soon return, even in their lifetimes, and bring about the fullness of God's kingdom on earth as it is in heaven. As time went by it eventually dawned on the early Christians that the world was not coming to an end as soon as they had expected. The second coming of Christ, the *parousia,* was being postponed, seemingly indefinitely. So they had to make plans for the long haul of history, living in the world, and not a very friendly one at that. Like everyone around them, they had to get up in the morning, feed the kids, get them off to school, go to work, undertake the chores of daily life, and assume responsibility for what is going on in the world around them.

When the first generation of Christians died out, the second generation had to deal with the question, How shall we live in the world? We have a letter preserved from this time written to a man whose name was Diognetus. This is how the author of the letter, whoever that might have been, described what it was like for Christians to live in the world:

> Christians are not distinguished from the rest of humanity by country, language, or custom. For nowhere do they live in cities of their own, nor do they speak some unusual dialect, nor do they practice an eccentric life-style. . . . But while they live in both Greek and Roman cities . . . they follow the local customs in dress and food and other aspects of life. At the same time they demonstrate remarkable and unusual character as citizens. They live in their own countries, but only as aliens. They participate in everything as citizens, and endure everything as foreigners. Every foreign country is their

fatherland, and every fatherland is foreign. They marry like everyone else, and they have children. . . . They share their food but not
their wives. They are "in the flesh," but they do not live "according
to the flesh." They live on earth but their citizenship is in heaven.
They obey the established laws; indeed, in their private lives they
transcend the laws of the land.[1]

The image of Christians as "aliens living in a foreign land" nicely cap-
tures the idea that Christians are to live "*in* but not *of* the world." But not
all Christians have come to the same conclusion regarding the most
faithful mode of being in the world. Fifty-some years ago H. Richard
Niebuhr wrote a little classic on the theme of this chapter entitled *Christ
and Culture*.[2] He showed that in the history of Christianity there are five
models of relationship between faith and politics, religion and society, or
church and state. At one extreme are those who set "Christ against culture." That leads to a sectarian strategy of withdrawal from the world
into separate communities. The Amish Christians try their best to do
that. They create a Christian enclave of their own apart from the wider
human community. At the other extreme is the "Christ of culture" model.
Christians of this type tend to be culture-conforming. They blur the distinction between the church and the world, between the biblical faith
and the "spirit of the age." The other three models represent typically
Catholic, Calvinist, and Lutheran ways of relating Christ and culture.
Niebuhr called the Catholic type "Christ above culture." That is best symbolized by the popes in the Middle Ages who claimed the right to crown
the emperor. These popes claimed absolute supremacy not only in the
church but in the world. The Calvinist type is called "Christ transforming
culture." The city of Geneva, Switzerland, in the sixteenth century was a
splendid example. It was an experiment to make the city Christian.
Geneva was run by Christian magistrates, its laws were written by Christians for Christians, and heretics were burned at the stake, which was
the fate of Servetus, who denied the Trinity.

1. "Letter to Diognetus," in *The Apostolic Fathers*, 2nd ed., tr. J. B. Lightfoot and J. R.
Hammer (Grand Rapids: Baker, 1989), pp. 296-306.
2. H. Richard Niebuhr, *Christ and Culture* (New York: Harper & Brothers Publishers,
1951).

Niebuhr's fifth type is the Lutheran view which he calls "Christ and culture in Paradox." This is more commonly referred to as the Lutheran doctrine of the two kingdoms of God. Luther's idea of the two kingdoms or two realms was his interpretation of what Augustine meant by the two cities of God, the earthly city and the heavenly city. The heavenly city refers to the Bible's depiction of salvation beginning with Adam and Eve in the Garden of Eden and ending with the vision of the saints in the heavenly city of Jerusalem. The road from paradise lost to paradise regained runs through the great cities built by the children of Cain: Babylon, Sodom, and Nineveh. Finally, Jerusalem becomes the battleground on which Christ defeats the "powers and principalities." The two kingdoms are also symbolized by Luther's idea of the two hands of God. The "left hand of God" — corresponding to Augustine's "earthly city" — was Luther's image of the way God administers the daily affairs of human life — marriage and family, political, economic, and cultural matters. God is at work in the secular realm through the structures of government and justice. For Luther God is always working incognito in and through instruments such as the laws of the state and the power of the sword to accomplish his will. The "right hand of God" is engaged in the events of world history to bring about the salvation of humankind. God does this through his covenant with Israel, the gospel of Christ, and the proclamation of the church, reaching out to the nations and peoples of the world.

The most difficult question is how the two kingdoms, the two cities, the two hands of God are related to each other. A common mistake is to completely separate them, maintaining that faith and politics have nothing to do with each other. One German theologian wrote: "The Gospel has absolutely nothing to do with public life but only with eternal life. . . . It is not the vocation of Jesus Christ or the Gospel to change the orders of secular life or to renew them. . . . Christianity wants to change a person's heart, not his social situation."[3] In the same vein a Lutheran jurist wrote that the issues of public life "should remain untouched by the proclamation of the Gospel, completely untouched."[4] "Dualism" is the word to de-

---

3. See Karl Hertz, ed., *Two Kingdoms and One World: A Sourcebook in Christian Social Ethics* (Minneapolis: Augsburg, 1976), p. 84.

4. Hertz, ed., *Two Kingdoms*, p. 87.

scribe this view. This means that when Christians enter public life, they must leave their personal faith behind. Such a dichotomy between a person's faith and the public square has no basis in the Bible or in Jesus' message and ministry. If it did, Jesus would not have been crucified by the Roman government, and John the Baptist would not have lost his head to King Herod. If faith is so private as to have no public expression, there would have been no Christian martyrs.

Heirs of the Reformation will recall that it began as an act of civil disobedience. Luther's faith was not so private as to keep him out of trouble with the civil authorities. He would not recant in face of the Emperor Charles V. His prince hid him away in the Wartburg Castle. And Luther made clear in his writings that there are times when it is necessary for a Christian to resist temporal authorities. It is necessary to break human laws when they violate the law of God. It is necessary to refuse to bear arms in a manifestly unjust war. Luther did not believe in an unconditional allegiance to the state, when the state commits acts against the law of God. There are times when a Christian must conscientiously object, even if it might mean going to prison or paying a fine or suffering the ridicule of one's peers. But we have to admit that not many church leaders have had the 20/20 vision to tell the difference between a just war and an unjust war, until long after the war is over. Patriotism or protest — sometimes it is hard for a Christian to decide which way to lean when one's nation beats its drums for war.

Most churches are deeply engaged with the question of the church's social responsibility. A large share of the agenda at every church-wide assembly is devoted to debates on issues that deal with the secular realm, issues of peace, justice, and the environment. Such matters having to do with the left hand of God are certainly important for Christians and churches, because they deal with the world that God created and sustains by his providential care. In this arena Christians stand shoulder to shoulder with people of other religious persuasions or humanists of no religion at all. They have to debate and deliberate the issues like everyone else, using their faculties of reason, conscience, and common sense with no apparent advantage. Still, Christians should remember that in this realm they are "resident aliens," with their ultimate loyalty lying elsewhere. "Seek ye first the kingdom of God and his righteousness and all these things will be added unto you" (Matt. 6:33). The priority for Christians must be with matters having to do with the right hand of God, things only they care about and are of no interest to non-Christians. The church's primary focus will be on matters of faith and evangelism, how to tell the gospel to people who have never heard, at home and abroad, how to plant new churches, and how to make new converts into literate witnesses. This means that when Christians get together in solemn assembly, they should give prime time to matters exclusive to the church as church and not merely play to the galleries of the world.

## The Way of Critical Participation

The eschatological kingdom that has *already* arrived in Jesus has *not yet* arrived to end the world. Thus, Christians live in the tension between the "already" and the "not yet." The ethical question for the church in the world is this: What should the community of the end time do in the meantime? There is a virtual ecumenical consensus that two extremes do not provide a proper answer. The one extreme is that of sectarian apocalypticism that says, "Let's not get involved in the world. The rapture will soon sweep us up into a cloud of other-worldly bliss." That was the ghastly experiment of Jonesville in Guyana (1978). The other extreme is that of a gnosticism that amalgamates Christianity with the science or wisdom of the age. Modern examples are Christian Science, the belief system founded by Mary Baker Eddy, and the Church of Scientology, the religion founded by L. Ron Hubbard.

The two kingdoms doctrine offers a middle way between the two extremes of separation from the world and identification with it. It teaches us the fine art of drawing a proper distinction between our Christian identity and our worldly involvement, between law and gospel, between justice and justification, between the left hand and the right hand of God. In the kingdom on the left we may strive for whatever kind of liberation is needed in any given situation. We may join a liberation movement, knowing full well that human liberation is not the same thing as Christian salvation. Some liberation theologians teach that liberation and salvation are two different words for the same thing. The two kingdoms doctrine spares us from making this mistake. No liberation movement can deliver the salvation that only Christ can give. The best government in the world cannot preach the gospel. The best possible social system cannot bestow the love of God and the forgiveness that only the gospel can offer. Freedom is one of the things our nation is willing to fight for, not only for itself but for other nations, as the United States did in the Second World War. But that kind of freedom must not be equated with that one thing needful — the freedom of the gospel for which Christ has set us free (Gal. 5:1). This is the freedom that the Apostle Paul enjoyed, even while sitting in shackles in a Philippian jail.

Some years ago a debate occurred in Germany on the question: "Must a Christian be a socialist?" Helmut Gollwitzer (1908-1993) said "yes," Christians must work for socialism. He did not, of course, mean Marxist communism. By socialism he had in mind a system of government that seeks economic equality and social justice for all. That would break down the huge gap between the rich and the poor, the haves and the have-nots, the owners and the workers, and so forth. Eberhard Jüngel said "no," Christians are free to be on the side of democratic capitalism. At this point the two kingdoms doctrine comes into play. It instructs us that it is wrong-headed to identify Christianity with socialism or with capitalism. The church should not pronounce a divine benediction on any social, economic, or political system. It is wrong to say in any election, "God is on our side" or to claim to know what Jesus would do. Again, the proper way is neither identification nor separation but critical participation. It is wrong for Christians to shirk their duty as citizens in the messy world of politics and economics. But it is equally wrong to claim that one's political affiliation is God's party, as some do in the heat of an election by recruiting religious activists for their partisan politics. The idea of critical participation means that one is not a flunky of any political party. One does not say, "My country, right or wrong." One does not believe, "Win at all costs." Critical participation is not lapdog but watchdog politics, the way of the Christian conscience cleansed by the gospel. Christians may exercise their freedom from captivity to any particular ideology, whether socialist or capitalist. If Christians are not to separate themselves from the world, they must choose the strategy of critical participation in every situation in which they find themselves and maintain a healthy suspicion of every system that does whatever it takes to keep the reins of power.

When Christians find themselves in a highly ambiguous situation, then it is salutary to remember Luther's counsel that they are "saints and sinners at the same time" *(simul iustus et peccator)*. Sometimes one faces no squeaky-clean option in the public square; one must choose between the lesser of two evils. If time proves that one has made a bad choice, it is not unforgivable. Christ did not die for the righteous, but for sinners.

Christians in Europe have organized from the left and the right to create their own political parties, be they Christian Socialist or Christian Democratic, or whatever. Frequently one hears that America is a Christian nation. Should not Christians band together to form a coalition to return America to the biblical values of its founding fathers? The First Amendment of the United States Constitution calls for the separation of church and state. Those who hold to the two kingdoms doctrine would be inclined to support it. But it all depends on how it is interpreted. Some interpret it to mean that it allows no expression of religion in the public realm. Religion belongs in the home and in church, but not in the public schools or political offices. Does the First Amendment prohibit prayer and Bible reading in public schools, or posting the Ten Commandments in a courtroom, or a public school choir singing a Christmas carol, or the President saying "God bless America" at the end of his speeches? Should we retain the words "under God" in the Pledge of Allegiance? Should the public square be denuded of all religious expressions and influences? The questions go on and on. Should there be chaplains in the U.S. military, with their salaries paid by tax dollars? Should there be a Christian chaplain in the U.S. Congress? If so, should a Jewish rabbi or a Muslim imam take their turns on a rotating basis? Should Christians try to create a moral majority to impose its norms on a secular pluralistic society? These are difficult and unresolved issues before the American public.

If we pray "God bless America," should we not pray that God would equally bless all nations? Are Americans the new "chosen people" elected by God to spread the gospel of democracy and free-market capitalism to all other nations? Just when Christian churches have for the most part stopped sending missionaries around the world in the name of Jesus, should they now endorse sending armies around the world in the name of democracy? Some years ago some Africans in the younger indigenous churches chanted the slogan, "Missionary, go home," so now not seldom do American tourists hear people yell out, "Yankee, go home."

The debate is ongoing about the place of religion in the public square. Organizations like the ACLU try to keep them separate. What is at stake for the Christian faith? Since we live in a religiously plural society, any religious expression in the public square will most assuredly represent not true Christianity but a watered-down civil religion. This means that at every invocation or benediction pronounced in a civil religious ritual, the name of the Triune God or Jesus Christ will be excluded and replaced by some abstract marshmallow deity. When civil religion is practiced in public places, it will usually be deistic or unitarian, but never really Christian. Do Christians really want to pray to a god other than the Father of Jesus Christ and intentionally omit ending a prayer with "in the name of Jesus"?

So the choices are rather grim. One option is to keep the public space completely secular. Get rid of "In God We Trust" and such shibboleths. That will make the ACLU and atheists happy. A second option is to join the celebrations of civil religion. But if we do that, do we not violate the First Amendment by consenting to an official establishment of a religion, namely, the American civil religion, which has its own sacred icons and rituals? A third option is to support the conservative evangelicals working to re-Christianize the civil religion. That would mean to fill public ceremonies with Christian rhetoric, with the result that non-Christians will feel like Jesus and the Bible are being rammed down their throats.

The practice of civil religion will not go away soon. Americans are an irrepressibly religious people. Not even the Supreme Court or Congress could prevent them from expressing their religious sentiments in times of national emergency like after the attacks of 9/11. Americans will sing "God bless America" as though it were their national anthem. On the Fourth of July, Thanksgiving Day, Memorial Day, and at the inauguration of Presidents, Americans will continue their practices of civil religion. We may think of this as the exercise of faith limited to the first article of the creed, minus any references to the second and third articles used in specifically Christian worship. Whether or to what extent a Christian may choose to join in such Christ-less ceremonies is a matter for each individual conscience. In a day and age when Christian faith is so readily confused with patriotic fervor, I think it wise for the church to discourage such participation.

Not all traditions adhere to the counsel to keep politics out of the pulpit. Roman Catholic priests are often called upon by their bishops to tell their parishioners how to vote and not to endorse candidates who disagree with the church's stance on particular issues. Black preachers have a strong tradition of bringing politics into the pulpit, as was brought to national attention in the case of the Rev. Jeremiah Wright. If we take our cue from the two kingdoms doctrine, a minister will preach the whole counsel of God, the Word of God in its twofold form, both law and gospel. He or she cannot preach simply the gospel. The gospel without the law is like an answer without a question or like taking medicine without a diagnosis.[5] In the kingdom on the left hand God rules through the law. In the kingdom on the right hand God rules through the gospel. It makes no sense to preach the gospel to AIG or General Motors or Microsoft or Haliburton. However, as custodians of the Word of God, both law and gospel, we do have the duty to preach the law of God and call for its observance in the secular world of business and government. That is the political use of the law.

Preachers have been called and ordained to preach the whole counsel of God, to announce both the demands of justice and the consolations of grace. When those who have been elected to uphold the just demands of the law act in lawless ways, they need to be called to account, even from the pulpit. When laws on the books prove to be manifestly unjust, it is right to call for their overthrow. What is the criterion? How can we tell when the law of God in the secular realm is being observed? We possess a critical standpoint in the idea of justice. The core of justice is

---

5. Consider what Martin Luther said about law and gospel: "Both the Law and the Gospel must be taught and considered. It is a mistake to confine yourself to one of the two. The Law serves no other purpose than to create a thirst and to frighten the heart. The Gospel alone satisfies the thirst, makes us cheerful, and revives and consoles the conscience." "Sermons on the Gospel of St. John, Chapters 6-8," *Luther's Works,* ed. Jaroslav Pelikan (Saint Louis: Concordia Publishing House, 1959), p. 272.

care for the neighbor. Justice is the form that love takes in the secular realm. The sum of the law is love of the neighbor. If we love our neighbors as ourselves, we will tend to the needs of our neighbors. That is what the story of the Good Samaritan is all about. The Good Samaritan did not preach the gospel to the victim by the roadside. He did what his neighbor needed, took him to an inn, paid the bill, and went on his way.

## Questions for Discussion

1. There were different movements in Palestine among the Jews in Jesus' day: Pharisees, Sadducees, Essenes, Zealots, and Herodians. Jesus did not belong to any of these movements, but how was he different from each of them?

2. What was so radical or revolutionary about the movement that Jesus started with his disciples? Give some examples of Jesus' radical message of the kingdom of God.

3. According to the apostle Paul, believers in Christ are to be "*in* but not *of* the world." That may be a good description of the life of a saint like St. Francis of Assisi, but may it not also be so of ordinary saints like the rest of us? What do you think?

4. Lutherans have taught the doctrine of the two kingdoms of God. Describe the two kingdoms, noting what is unique to each and how they are different.

5. Do you think Christians should be involved in politics or political parties? If so, do you think their Christian faith should inform them about what political choices to make?

6. What is your reaction to hearing political opinions and convictions preached from the pulpit, whether from the right or from the left?

7. Do you think it is helpful to ask "What would Jesus do?" when facing a difficult ethical decision on social, economic, or political matters?

# *Conclusion*

The questions and answers in this book concerning Jesus of Nazareth
have taken us on a long journey, beginning with the Bible, proceed-
ing through the centuries of the Christian tradition, and culminating in
what various present-day historians and theologians are saying. The history of Christology abounds with conflict and controversy, as thoughtful
people have attempted to answer Jesus' question, "Who do people say
that I am?" After two thousand years, that question continues to evoke
the wildest assortment of contradictory answers from scholars who
have devoted a good share of their lives to discover who Jesus really was
in the days of his flesh.

Many of the questions we have posed in this book go back to the first
generation of Christian theologians who found it necessary to reflect on
their faith in Jesus. The question and answer method we have used is a
simple version of the more sophisticated method used by the medieval
scholastics to teach the disciplines of law, theology, the arts, and medicine. It is known as scholastic disputation, or *quaestio disputata*. Thomas
Aquinas elevated the use of this method to the highest perfection in dealing with the disputed questions *(quaestiones disputatae)* in his teaching
about the truth, the soul, the power of God, and similar topics.

My guess is that every educated Christian layperson has asked the
questions of this book in some way or other. It is hardly possible to hear
sermons Sunday after Sunday from thoughtful preachers and to be an
active participant in programs of adult Christian education without

wondering who Jesus is, how we come to know him today, what he means for our life and salvation, and how we should witness to him in our conversations with non-Christian friends and neighbors.

This little book is a kind of apologetic for ordinary Christian lay folks who have not had the luxury of a formal theological education. Every chapter ends with "questions for discussion," to help the teacher focus on the main points. My hope is that pastors will take the time to teach their people the church's understanding of Jesus' identity and meaning. The news media loves to circulate the most sensational stories about Jesus, imagined by people who care neither for the gospel nor for the church. Laypeople who hear these stories need some help to sort out the truth from all the baseless rumors.

For the sake of full disclosure, the answers in this book have been constructed unabashedly in sync with the classical creeds and dogmas of the church. Over time these have proved to be the most trustworthy signposts along the journey of inquiry into the most difficult theological topics. If theologians do not use these signposts from the Christian tradition, they will inevitably use others, perhaps appealing to scientific reason or personal experience, or perhaps to some ideological commitment or other religious perspective. Books written about Jesus continue to be among the bestsellers. They promise new visions of Jesus and are read with great enthusiasm. They will suffer the same fate as all the others, soon to be forgotten, if they contribute nothing of lasting value for the edification and devotion of men and women who believe in Jesus Christ and carry out the mission of his church.

Perceptive readers will wonder, why just these questions? There are many others that are worthy of serious consideration. Here are a few that come to mind. Is the story of Jesus' birth of the Virgin Mary myth or history? What does it mean to confess in the creed that Jesus went to hell? Does it matter for the Christian faith that Jesus was a Jew? What can we know about the last things, such as, the Second Coming, the millennium, the resurrection of all the dead, the final judgment, the end of the world, etc.? Might it not be a useful learning experience for members of the class each to formulate a question about Jesus, construct an answer, and then share with the class? The essays could be bound together and kept as a supplement to the questions and answers treated in this little book.

# Index of Names

Abelard, 101
Anselm, 99, 100
Apollinaris, 65, 67
Aquinas, Thomas, 141
Arius, 62, 65-66
Athanasius, 62, 65-67
Augustine, 54, 99, 132
Aulén, Gustaf, 101

Bachmann, E. Theodore, 42
Baha'u'llah, 77
Barth, Karl, 9, 12, 16, 25, 42, 86-87
Bartsch, Hans W., 13
Bauckham, Richard, 23
Bergendoff, Conrad, 115
Bethge, Eberhard, 96, 107
Beveridge, Henry, 34
Bockmuehl, Markus, 23
Bonhoeffer, Dietrich, 96, 107
Borg, Marcus, 13, 18, 20-22, 25, 28-29, 38, 44, 68
Bornkamm, Günther, 1, 14-16, 25
Braaten, Carl E., 2, 8-9, 15-16, 75
Brandon, S. G. F., 21
Braun, Herbert, 15
Brown, Dan, 117
Brunner, Emil, 9
Bultmann, Rudolf, 2, 9, 12-16, 43, 64

Calvin, John, 33-34, 70
Conzelmann, Hans, 14-15, 18
Crossan, John Dominic, 2, 18-22, 38, 44
Cullmann, Oscar, 42
Cyprian, 36

Diderot, 21
Diem, Hermann, 10
Diognetus, 130
Driver, Tom, 73
Dunn, James D. G., 23

Ebeling, Gerhard, 14-17
Eddy, Mary Baker, 134
Edwards, Jonathan, 55
Erasmus of Rotterdam, 70
Eutyches, 65, 67
Evans, Craig A., 23

Fiorenza, Elizabeth Schüssler, 22
Forde, Gerhard, 94
Francis of Assisi, 128, 139
Fuchs, Ernst, 14-15
Fuller, Reginald F., 13
Funk, Robert, 18-19, 21-22, 35, 38, 44-45, 51, 119-20, 125

Gautama Buddha, 28, 36, 90-91, 98, 106

## Index of Names

Schweitzer, Albert, 1, 2, 8, 10, 15, 20-21, 29, 39-40
Scobie, Andrew, 16
Smith, Louise P., 14
Smith, Morton, 21
Smith, Ronald G., 16
Spong, John, 22
Strauss, David, F., 7, 38, 49-50

Talbert, Charles H., 49
Tappert, Theodore G., 29
Tertullian, 40, 118
Tetzel, John, 100
Theissen, Gerd, 22
Thiering, Barbara, 22
Thomas, M. M., 89
Thomson, G. T., 9

Tillich, Paul, 2, 9-10, 13, 16, 25, 38, 43
Tyrell, George, 8

Updike, John, 87

Vermes, Geza, 22
Vivekananda, Swami, 76
Voltaire, 21

Walker, Adrian, 23
Wedderburn, A. J. M., 50
Wingren, Gustaf, 86
Wright, Jeremiah, 138
Wright, N. T., 2, 6, 23, 25, 31-32, 38, 68-69
Wyon, Olive, 9

# Index of Subjects

# Index of Subjects

Jesus Seminar, 2, 5, 11, 18-22, 26-29, 35, 38, 44-45, 51, 111, 119

Jews, 42, 60, 87-88, 112

Judaism, 22, 77, 88, 117

Justification, 30, 134

Kerygma, 12-16, 24, 45

Kingdom of God, 91, 106, 109-10, 120, 124, 127-29, 133, 139

Law, 99, 102, 133, 138

Liberal Protestantism, 8, 17, 33, 37, 53, 55, 64, 101, 121

Liberation, 134-35

Living Christ, 25, 37, 42, 50

Lord's Supper, 19, 70-72, 112, 116, 123

Love, 83, 105, 122, 139

Metaphysics, 71, 95

Ministry, 116, 124

Miracles, 7, 10, 21, 23

Missionaries, 80, 100, 113, 123, 136

Monophysitism, 67

Muslims, 36, 46, 69, 87-89, 104

Orthodox Christianity, 85, 124

Patripassianism, 107

Pluralistic Theory of Religions, 76-79, 82, 85

Politics, 127-39

Preaching, 35-38, 40-41, 43, 81-82, 122, 135

Predestination, 84, 86

Ransom, 98-101

Real Jesus, 11, 25, 27, 30, 46

Reason, 31-32, 37

Religion, Religions, 36, 72, 75-78, 80-87, 100, 136-37

Resurrection, 7, 10, 13, 17-18, 34, 36, 46, 49-57, 60-61, 85-86, 95, 105-6, 108, 111-12, 119-20, 130

Revelation, 17, 31-32, 42, 44, 79-80

Roman Catholicism, 39, 70, 100

Sacraments, 35, 37, 52, 122

Salvation, 10, 30, 36, 38, 42, 44, 60, 61-63, 66-73, 75, 79, 81-86, 90, 97, 108, 118-19, 129, 132

Satisfaction theory, 99-101, 106

Sin, 10, 55, 93, 98, 100, 103, 105

Sinners, 34, 97-98, 105-6, 136

Suffering, 95, 97, 105, 129

Trinity, 61, 67, 83, 89, 113, 116, 131, 137

Truth, 32, 141

Two kingdoms of God, 132, 135

Universalism, 56, 85-86

Word of God, 12-13, 43, 113, 123, 138

Worship, 20, 41, 63, 124, 138